a **WEE GUIDE** *to*
Old Churches *and*
Abbeys *of* Scotland

a **WEE GUIDE** *to*
Old Churches *and* Abbeys *of* Scotland

Martin Coventry
Joyce Miller

GOBLINSHEAD

Edinburgh

First Published 1997
© Martin Coventry 1997
Text © Martin Coventry & Joyce Miller 1997
Published by **GOBLINSHEAD**
12 Merchiston Crescent
Edinburgh EH10 5AS
Scotland

British Library Cataloguing in Publication Data
A catalogue record for this book is available from the British Library.

ISBN 1 899874 09 7

Typeset by **GOBLINSHEAD** using Desktop Publishing
Typeset in Garamond Narrow

a **WEE GUIDE** *to*
Old Churches *and*
Abbeys *of* Scotland

Contents

List of illustrations

Acknowledgements

Thanks to everyone who had a hand in the book, especially to
Sir J C Stormonth-Darling and Scotland's Churches Scheme for supplying
such useful information about many of the sites. Their handbook,
Churches to Visit in Scotland in 1997, is packed with information about
churches to visit – both old and new – and is excellent value at £1.50
from bookshops.

How to use this book

This book is divided into two main parts:

- The first part (pages 3–21) is an overview of the development of Christianity in Scotland.
- The second part (pages 23–78) lists over 120 churches, abbeys, chapels, crosses and other Christian monuments. A map, covering two pages (pages 24–5), locates every site. Each entry begins with the name of the church or site, its location, and then its National Grid Reference and Ordnance Sheet Landranger number. This is followed by a description of the site. The final part covers opening – where available – with telephone numbers and facilities, including parking, refreshments, sales area, admission, WC, and disabled facilities.

The glossary of terms (pages 79–82), includes a simple plan layout of an abbey, a collegiate church, a cathedral and a parish church; and a description of the different Christian communities (pages 83–4), concludes this section.

An index (pages 85–8) lists all the sites, people and events alphabetically.

Warning

While the information in this book was believed to be correct at time of going to press – and was checked, where possible, with the visitor attractions – opening times and facilities, or other information, may vary or differ from that included. All information should be checked with the visitor attractions before embarking on any journey. Inclusion in the text is no indication whatsoever that a site is open to the public or that it should be visited. Many sites, particularly ruined churches and abbeys, are potentially dangerous and great care should be taken: the publisher and authors cannot accept responsibility for damage or injury caused from any visit.

The places listed to visit are only a personal selection of what is available in Scotland, and the inclusion or exclusion of a visitor attraction in the text should not be considered as a comment or judgement on that attraction.

Locations on the map are approximate.

Introduction

Because places of worship were so fundamentally important to society, often just reading about them can be a bit unsatisfactory. It is usually more atmospheric – as well as interesting – to visit sites in person, as the location and surroundings are as significant as the buildings themselves. Whether the weather be glorious or gloomy, bright sunshine or dark rain clouds, we have found each site has its own particular mood and feeling, and we hope that this book gives an impression of something of the interest and variety of Chtistian sites which are found in Scotland.

From the simplest parish church to the most sophisticated cathedral, from gloomy Torphichen Preceptory to the light and peace of Iona, the guide includes a concise history of the development of worship in Scotland, both architecturally and ceremonially, from the earliest times to the 17th century. This is followed by a gazetteer of some 120 sites – which we think are both accessible and worth visiting – illustrating some of the common features of early churches, abbeys and other monuments. However, our selection remains a personal one, and in a work as small as this it was not possible to include as many sites as we would have liked.

MC & JM, Edinburgh, April 1997

Worship in Scotland

THE STONES OF TIME

The story of religion and worship in Scotland is as old as the people themselves, although what form this took in ancient times is speculative. Numerous standing stones, stone circles and burial cairns can be found all over the country, but the beliefs that shaped their construction and form have been lost. And despite excavation, plotting of grid references, geophysics, radiocarbon dating and other forms of investigation the definitive answer is likely to be elusive.

Chambered cairns and funerary mounds are found in many parts of Scotland, as well as other parts of Europe. Chambered cairns may have been single- or multi-chambered: several chambers opening off a central passageway; or a larger single chamber divided into stalls. Many of the sites were used and reused over thousands of years.

Stone circles, henges, and single and groupings of stones were built as early as 5000 years ago. Some have burial sites within their circumference; others are surrounded by a ditch – a henge monument; while others have a recumbent stone between two uprights, examples of which are found in Grampian. Callanish, on the island of Lewis, is at the centre of a complex site of circles and groupings of stones. The main

Callanish Stones, Lewis

stones are arranged in a cross-shaped pattern, and the site is believed to be a lunar observatory.

Indeed, a common belief is that the circles had some relationship to astrological cycles and changes, and their positions were significant

3

indicators of notable lunar and solar events – although the evidence from many sites does not confirm this theory. Whatever, pragmatism and spiritual requirements were probably closely linked. It seems unlikely that Stone Age man would build such structures without solid practical – as well as religious – reasons.

The purpose of single standing stones, or pairs, is even harder to determine. Some may have had a relationship with a nearby circle, others may have been marking stones of territory or an important place for local communities, while others were probably placed on the site of a battle or burial. Later generations developed rituals and uses for these stones of their own, including healing and magic – to cure toothache or enhance fertility: practices which would be condemned by the Reformed church in the 16th century.

EARLY CHRISTIAN WORSHIP – SAINTS AND LEGENDS

As the centuries passed, the religious beliefs of the societies which inhabited the land adapted and altered. Picts, Britons, Romans, Angles and Vikings all expanded or lost territory, and beliefs and customs introduced by one were assimilated into the culture of others.

By the time of the Roman invasion of Britain, 79 to 84 AD, written accounts record that the inhabitants of these islands were Druids. Although some of the Roman invaders of Britain were Christian, they appear to have made little attempt to introduce Christianity to the general population.

This was left to Ninian in 430 AD, after the Roman legions had been recalled. He had been educated at Rome, was a disciple of St Martin of Tours, and founded a religious house at Whithorn – *Candida Casa*. This monastic form of house was organised into cells, for the monks; agricultural work to provide food; and evangelistic work by way of missionary work in order to convert pagans to Christianity. There were three sites at Whithorn: the diocesan centre at *Candida Casa*; the monastery on the Isle of Whithorn; and a hermitage at Physgill, now known as St Ninian's Cave.

At much the same time Irish missionaries travelled from Bangor to the west of Scotland, including St Moluag and St Maelrubha. These two set up places of worship at Lismore and Applecross, but were independent of Whithorn.

By the 6th century, many Scots travelled from Ireland and settled in Argyll, their kingdom known as Dalriada. Irish religious organisation was arranged by family or tribe association, rather than with a geographical area, and in 563 Columba – who was of the Irish royal family of Ui Neill – settled on Iona, which may have been a Druidical centre. Like Ninian, he

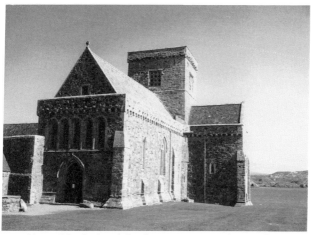

Iona Abbey – Columba founded a Christian community here in 563.

developed an organisation which combined monasticism and missionary work.

Near Inverness, Columba converted the northern Picts, ruled by Bridei or Brude, to Christianity. The story associated with this conversion is that Columba had a trial of power with one of the king's magi at Loch Ness. Indeed, the first account of a creature in Loch Ness is also related at this time, as Columba is said to have saved a servant from the monster.

Iona became the main centre of Celtic Christianity in Scotland, and more is known about Columba than many of his other contemporaries because of the work of Adamnan, another Irish monk, who arrived at Iona about 673. During his time as abbot, Adamnan wrote the *Vita Sancti Columbae* in which he included the many miraculous stories connected with Columba.

About this time (?520-612) Kentigern, also known as Mungo, did missionary work in Cumbria and south-west Scotland. Legend has it that his mother was Thenew, or Enoch, who was cast out by her father, the king of Lothian. After being placed in a coracle, she arrived a Culross, in Fife, where she was taken in by St Serf. Her son was raised by Serf, and was later sent as a missionary to the west, around the Clyde and Glasgow

Glasgow Cathedral – crypt

area. Although it is recorded that he met Columba, little else is known about his life apart from myths and legends. St Mungo's shrine is in the crypt of Glasgow Cathedral.

PARTING OF THE WAYS – ROMAN VERSUS CELTIC CHRISTIANITY

By 635 two Northumbrian princes, Oswald and Oswin, were exiled in Dalriada, and during time spent on Iona converted to Christianity. On their return to Northumbria, Aidan, a missionary from Iona, followed them and established Lindisfarne, Melrose and Coldingham as Christian communities. His work was continued by Cuthbert, who had been a novice at Melrose.

Cuthbert eventually became prior, and later bishop, of Lindisfarne, but also took time to live as a hermit on St Cuthbert's Isle and the Farne Islands. During his time as prior of Lindisfarne, the practices of the Celtic and Roman forms of worship were debated at the Synod of Whitby in 664. The differences between the two forms included the dating of Easter, and the necessity of tonsure, but the fundamental argument was between Episcopal and monastic organisation.

In Celtic monastic organisation a bishop was subordinate to an abbot, but with an Episcopal organisation bishops were head of, and superior to, all in a diocesan area. The Roman form of organisation was accepted, although Colman, who had represented the Celtic argument at Whitby, and others returned to Iona where they maintained an independent organisation until 716.

Another major site of religious settlement was St Andrews where St Rule, thought to be a disciple of Columba, established a community about 590 – the site later occupied by the Cathedral. In 733 Acca, bishop of Hexham, brought the relics of St Andrew to Fife. Lindisfarne, Iona and St Andrews became centres for Christian stone carving, and the magnificent High Crosses of Kildalton and Iona date from this time, while the cross at Ruthwell dates from the 7th century.

In 793 the main coastal religious sites of Iona and Lindisfarne suffered the first of several attacks by the Vikings. In 806, 68 monks were reputedly slaughtered. Iona was abandoned in 826, and some of the community – with Kenneth MacAlpin's encouragement – moved to the safer location of Dunkeld. Cuthbert's relics were taken from Lindisfarne to Durham.

There is little documentary evidence of this period apart from the Irish Annals, but it is known that at this time certain of the relics held at Iona were separated, perhaps for safe keeping. The manuscript, inscribed on Iona, which would later be known as the *Book of Kells* was taken to Kells, County Meath in Ireland. The shrine of St Columba was removed to Dunkeld. A carved wooden box, decorated with bronze and semi-precious stones, known as the *Monymusk Reliquary* or the *Breccbennach* was said to have contained a relic of bone from Columba. It is now in the National Museum of Scotland, Edinburgh.

With the removal from Iona, the Irish and Scottish Churches became increasingly separate. Dunkeld was for a time regarded as the centre of the Scottish Church, but was eventually replaced by St Andrews. The bishops of St Andrews were known as *Episcopus Scottorum* – chief bishop of Scotland, but were not granted archbishopric status by Rome. This became a serious problem during the wars with England in the 13th and 14th centuries, as the English Church – as well as Edward I – claimed superiority over their northern neighbour.

MONKS AND MONASTERIES – THE ARRIVAL OF RELIGIOUS ORDERS

During the reign of Malcolm Canmore, his queen, Margaret, made major contributions to the Church in Scotland. She was very involved with both the secular and religious trends of the period, and was critical of what she saw as laxness in the organisation of the Church, including the lack of diocesan structure.

To this end, she started a Benedictine monastery at Dunfermline in

1072, and revived the monastery on Iona. More importantly she laid the foundations of Church reform that her son David would continue. Margaret herself was reported – by her devoted biographer Turgot – to have been a pious and practical Christian. She provided care for the poor, notably a ferry to cross the Firth of Forth for those undertaking a pilgrimage to St Andrews. Margaret was canonised in 1250, and her chapel in Edinburgh Castle was built by her son, David.

In Ireland as early as the 8th century *Keledei, Celi Dé* or *Culdees* - friends of God – set up isolated religious communities. Several of these

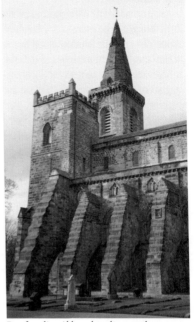

Dunfermline Abbey church – see above

arrived in Scotland and set up monasteries at Abernethy, Brechin, Loch Leven and Monifieth, as well as St Andrews and elsewhere. Although Margaret had respect for the piety of these communities, their independence was gradually eroded as they became incorporated into, or replaced by, continental forms of monasticism.

David I continued his mother's reforms in a number of ways, both at parish and higher level. In order to provide for a church and priest in every parish, teinds or tithes – a payment of 10% of annual income – were introduced. He organised and divided the kingdom into 10 bishoprics, although there were actually 13 within the boundaries of modern Scotland, re-establishing old dioceses and introducing a new one in Caithness. Galloway remained under the control of York. The dioceses of Orkney and Sodor – the Western Isles – were under Norwegian rule, the Archbishopric of Nidaros or Trondheim: Sodor until the late 13th century, and Orkney until 1383.

The dioceses which were re-introduced by David, and his heir Alexander I, all had cathedrals: Dunblane, Glasgow, Aberdeen, Brechin, Dunkeld, Elgin, Fortrose, St Andrews, Whithorn and Dornoch. Whithorn and St Andrews were monastic, and had priories attached, while the others had secular canons.

ORDER AND DESIGN – DAILY ROUTINE AND RITUAL

The daily order and life of the religious houses was strictly controlled and based on Roman rite, although local variations were introduced by way of dedications to native saints, particularly in the 15th century. There were usually seven services per day, with the high mass being the main celebration.

The architectural plan of medieval cathedrals was fairly standard. The main area – the choir and presbytery – was for the celebration of the religious services by the clergy; but there was an area – the nave – for lay people to congregate and observe at least some of the major festivals.

The main axis (for all churches) was east to west, and the high alter was at the east end. An area, near the altar – called the choir – was where the canons were positioned during the service; and the lay congregation remained in the west end – the nave. There were sometimes projecting wings, at right angles – transepts – in which there were smaller altars to saints. The presbytery, at the east end of the choir, held the bishop's throne and stalls for the canons and other important people. The nave and choir were separated by a screen – a rood screen – often highly carved, the finest surviving example is in Glasgow Cathedral.

Glasgow and Kirkwall are the only two cathedrals which survived the Reformation intact. Brechin, Dunblane, Dunkeld, Dornoch, Iona, Lismore, and Aberdeen continue to be used as parish churches, and have been repaired, re-modelled and sympathetically (at least latterly) restored as needed. Elgin, St Andrews, and Whithorn are all ruinous, but the size and layout can be determined from the remains of the foundations.

David I founded many houses of continental religious orders. The Benedictines had been introduced by Margaret. David introduced Cluniac Benedictines at Newcastle and Crossraguel, and Cistercians at Melrose in 1136. He also founded a house of Tironensian canons at Selkirk in 1113, although it later moved to Kelso.

It was not only the Crown which introduced religious orders to Scotland. The Valliscaulians Order was introduced at Ardchattan by Duncan MacDougall, Lord Lorne in 1230. Alexander I, David I's brother, had founded an order of Augustinian canons at Scone in 1120, which spread to many houses including Cambuskenneth, Inchcolm, Loch Leven and St Andrews. The Premonstratensian order of canons was introduced at Dryburgh, again by David, and there were eventually six houses, including Whithorn. There were also Trinitarian houses in Scotland, including one at Peebles.

David I introduced Anglo-Norman building style with its Romanesque features of rounded arches and windows. The overall pattern was more squared and squat to provide the stability and support for heavy walls and vaulted stone ceilings. Chevron – zigzag – ornamentation over door arches is a distinct Norman feature. Good examples of Romanesque design can be seen at Dalmeny, Leuchars, St Margaret's chapel in Edinburgh Castle, and the Abbey church at Dunfermline.

In the mid to late 12th century, Gothic style of architecture was introduced. With improved building techniques, such as buttressing, this style allowed for more decorative, lighter designs. The use of pointed arches and windows meant there could be both more, and larger, windows decorated with tracery. Vaults were higher with concave arches.

St Margaret's Chapel, Edinburgh Castle

Although little is left at St Andrews, some idea of size and scale of its Gothic design can be seen from the ruins. Dundrennan Abbey, in Kirkcudbright, illustrates a hybrid design. Building started in a Romanesque style, but later re-modelling and additions had tall, pointed Gothic arches. Jedburgh and Arbroath abbeys are fine examples of late-Gothic style, although these buildings took so long to construct and required frequent repair – especially after English attacks – that very often they incorporate a variety of different styles.

By the 13th century, other orders had been founded in Europe in reaction to the excesses of wealth and ornamentation to which some in the Church were prone. These begging, or mendicant orders, were founded by St Francis and St Dominic, and located their orders near towns in order to preach to the laity. These orders, the Dominicans – Blackfriars – and Franciscans – Greyfriars – reached Scotland about 1230, and set up friaries around towns such as Edinburgh, Perth, St Andrews, Dundee, Glasgow, Montrose, Ayr, Dumfries, Inverness and many others. Because these orders had their establishments in towns, few of the Friary buildings remain standing: many were singled out for destruction at the Reformation.

Monastic life was standardised. The religious day was much like cathedral worship with eight services or 'hours' on ordinary days. As monastic communities grew, there was an increased number and variety of special roles for the monks – cooks, gardeners, care of the sick, music, the writing of manuscripts, as well as the administration and overseeing of the large amounts of feudal lands which the monasteries held. Many establishments also had lay-brothers, who assisted in the more menial tasks around the abbey.

The plan of monastic churches was similar to the cathedrals, and they were located on the north side of the cloister. The other monastic buildings – the domestic buildings – were located to the south side of the church, forming a rectangle known as a cloister. These included the refectory, the dormitory and the chapter house. Often there would be a passageway and stairs leading from the dormitory into the church, so the monks did not have to go outside when they attended services at night. There would also be a parlour; warming room; kitchen; infirmary; cellars as well as accommodation for lay-brothers; guest accommodation; store-rooms; bake-houses and brew-houses.

The best-preserved complex of domestic buildings can be found at Inchcolm, while substantial parts of the church can been seen at Jedburgh and Melrose. The nave at Dunfermline abbey continued to be used as a parish church after the Reformation, but the remains of the domestic buildings, like Dryburgh and Melrose, give an impression of the size and layout. The body of Robert the Bruce, Robert I, is buried at Dunfermline, while his heart was interred at Melrose. The casket, believed to contain his heart, has recently been examined then re-interred by Historic Scotland.

The Tironensian abbey at Arbroath was founded by William the Lion in 1178, and although it is ruinous, is of significance because of its contribution during the Wars on Independence. Some of the walls of the south transept, the west towers and the presbytery and sacristy can still be seen. The roofed Abbot's house dates from the 15th or 16th centuries, but does incorporate earlier building, and now houses a museum. In 1320 a letter was sent to Pope John XXII, drafted by Abbot Bernard de Linton of Arbroath. This letter, which would later be known as the *Declaration of Arbroath,* complained about the repeated harassment of the Scots by the English. The Scottish Church was determined to remain independent and would support Robert the Bruce in his attempt to defeat Edward of England.

Another abbey which is associated with this period of Scottish history is Sweetheart Abbey in Dumfriesshire. It was established in 1273, as a daughter house of the Cistercian abbey at Dundrennan, by Devorgilla the wife of John Balliol, whose son was King John I *Toom Tabard.* Devorgilla's husband had died four years previously, and the abbey was established to his memory. She had his heart embalmed and placed in an ivory casket, and when she died in 1290, the casket was buried beside her in the sanctuary of the monastery: her stone

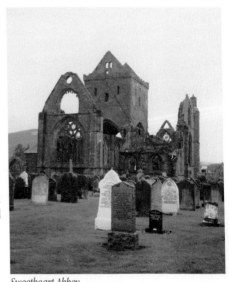
Sweetheart Abbey

effigy survives, although it has been defaced. The name Sweetheart – or *Dulce Cor* – was chosen to signify her eternal love. There are substantial, though unroofed, remains of the church and much of the precinct wall is visible. There is little left of the domestic buildings.

The majority of the population, however, did not worship in such buildings. Small simple rectangular churches, divided into chancel and nave, often with a thatched roof, were commonplace in small parishes.

Relationship with Rome – National and International Trends

Surviving liturgies from the 13th to 16th centuries show that the form of
service worshipped in Scotland did not vary much from the Roman ritual.
The *filia specialis* relationship which had been granted by Rome, after
the Wars of Independence, had removed any attempt at Episcopal
interference by York and established a direct relationship with Rome. But
no Scottish archbishopric had been created, and with the wars and after
there was increased deviation between the two.

   The *Great Schism* within the Western church of 1378-1418 was but one
of the many ways the two Churches differed. Also, although the liturgy
used in Scotland was based on that of Salisbury – Sarum – there were a
number of features which were more continental than English. Clerical
dress, church furnishings, and differences in ceremonial procedure
illustrated the Scottish Church's direct relationship with Rome. The host
was raised and censed during services, and the sacrament was stored in a
monstrance, or Eucharist – an elaborate container – which was then kept
in a sacrament house between services.

   It was during the 15th century that Scotland was granted two
archbishoprics: St Andrews in 1472, and Glasgow in 1492. In the same
century, other continental trends in religious worship found popularity in
Scotland: new cults such as Holy Blood; the Passion; the Five Wounds;
while there was also an increase in dedications and re-dedications to
native Scottish saints.

   Pilgrimages to sites in Spain and Italy were popular, but there were
also major sites in Scotland. Originally native saints had been worshipped
at local shrines, but some relics were moved and relocated to larger
churches or cathedrals, or larger churches were built for them. These
included St Machar at Aberdeen, St Mungo or Kentigern at Glasgow, St
Duthac at Tain, St Mirren at Paisley, and St Ninian at Whithorn.

   Not only were the relics of local saints venerated, but the liturgies and
services held introduced new feasts and ceremonies into the religious
calendar. There are surviving breviaries from this time which show that
there were numerous feast days for Scottish, Irish or Northumbrian
saints, as well as other major saints' days. The breviary from Fowlis Easter
includes seven Scottish saints, and the *Arbuthnott Missal* six .

   By the time of Bishop Elphinstone – Bishop of Aberdeen between
1483-1514 – the yearly liturgy was so overcrowded and disorganised that

he commissioned a new *Aberdeen Breviary*, which he intended would become the national calendar. English material was removed – except for Northumbrian saints – and the ceremonies were standardised. His attempt to unify national worship was not successful, however, as, by the time his breviary was printed, Rome had brought out a new standard: the Quinonez breviary.

Apart from the official church worship conducted by clerics, there was an increasing fashion for personal piety in the 15th and 16th centuries. As mentioned, cults such as the Holy Blood and the Rosary became popular, as did dedicating altars and collegiate churches to favourite or patron saints. These were institutions in which a number of secular clergy were provided for by an endowment, but the clergy administered themselves. The purpose of the college was to ensure the saying of prayers and masses for the dead in perpetuity.

Many of these churches were founded in rural areas, near the lands or household of the lay patron. Some of the early colleges had royal patronage, but the majority were provided for by wealthy magnates. Others were located in towns, and were provided for by their councils. These buildings were all built to unique plans, and became increasingly ornate, as they became symbols of status and wealth.

Some fine examples remain at Rosslyn, Seton, Restalrig, Chapel Royal and the Holy Rude at Stirling, Dunglass, Lincluden, Bothwell, Cullen and

Dunglass Collegiate Church

Innerpeffray. Many of these churches had aisled naves and transepts, and were built in a cruciform shape.

REJECTION OF ROME – REFORMING IDEAS

At the same time, new Reforming ideas arrived in Scotland from the Continent and England. The Roman Church was denounced as corrupt, morally and spiritually, and despite attempts at reform from within both within Scotland and by the Papacy, the ideas of Calvin and Luther found support and following, particularly in areas like Perth, Dundee and Edinburgh.

Although there were some individuals executed as martyrs – George Wishart was burnt by Cardinal Beaton in 1546 – the Reformation in Scotland was remarkable for its relative lack of violence. In 1557 the *First Bond* was signed by several earls and lords, which declared their intention to overthrow the Roman Church.

There were episodes of open hostility, and many friaries and churches were damaged or destroyed. The Reformers eventually achieved their goal when Scotland was declared a Protestant country in 1560, and abbeys and priories were dissolved, their land and property going to the Crown. The bold statement of their hopes for the Church – the *Confession of Faith* – by the Reformation parliament was however, both rather ambitious and of dubious legality. The Church had no official policy, structure or financial settlement, and although the *First Book of Discipline* – a 'mission statement', declaring their aims for the new church, including organisation, education and practice – was drafted and accepted, lack of trained ministers meant that a well-organised national church would not evolve until almost a century later.

No account of these events would be complete without mentioning John Knox. Ordained as a priest, he was much influenced by George Wishart, and joined Cardinal Beaton's murderers at St Andrews Castle during the siege there. He was taken prisoner by the French, but between 1549 and 1553 established a reputation in England for preaching radical Protestant ideas. During his time in Geneva, he was influenced by the ideas of John Calvin, and in 1555 made a preaching tour in Scotland, where he found support from many lords and landowners. He returned to Scotland during the final years of Mary of Guise's Regency, and was involved in the drafting of the *First Book of Discipline*.

Although the motives for rejecting the Roman form of worship may have been spiritual, for some political and economic reasons were equally important. It was true that later Stewart monarchs – James IV and James V – had perhaps abused the royal prerogative that had been granted to James III. This allowed the Crown to make their own appointments, and as a result several natural sons of the Stewart kings had been promoted to lucrative positions in the Church. However, the monarchs were not alone in benefiting from this system as quite a few other families of the Scottish nobility also 'acquired' the revenue of ecclesiastical properties by appointing commendators from their own families. Commendators were originally clerics who carried out the administrative work of the benefices, but by the 16th century some were laymen. After the Reformation, former Church lands were parcelled out to the nobility.

Equally relevant to the progress of the Reformation were the political relations between Protestant England, Catholic France, and Scotland. It was ultimately English intervention on the side of the Protestant party which helped to bring about the 1560 declaration; but it was also the Francophile policies of Mary of Guise which had alienated some of the Scottish nobles.

The *Confession of Faith* abolished the Latin mass and papal supremacy; rejected transubstantiation; reduced the number of sacraments to two; and stressed the importance of the vernacular in preaching, education and instruction. Also there was to be increased participation by the laity, in worship, administration and congregational discipline. To this 'democratic' end, a hierarchy of church committees was formed – kirk, presbytery, synod and General Assembly – where there would be clerical and lay representation. Although this organisation was formed in theory, it took many years before presbyteries were properly up and running.

There were just as many problems with the training of Reformed ministers; supervision of the different areas; and the financial settlement of the Church. The Church continued to rely heavily on the Crown for financial support, and for the rest of the century and into the next there was a long debate about their relationship. This would eventually result in the re-introduction of bishops by Charles I, leading to further bloodshed over religion, but during the heady days of post-1560 Scotland certain aspects of the new Church were greeted enthusiastically.

The removal of idolatrous monuments and religious images, as well as the abolishment of veneration of relics, meant that the majority of pre-Reformation churches continued to be used after being cleared. Some

churches, however, were built to a new design – notably Burntisland
Parish church, which was build in 1595; and Greyfriars in Edinburgh.
Burntisland was the first post-Reformation church in Scotland, built to a
solid square plan. The act of worship was to be a congregate act with no
barrier between the minister and congregation: no rood screen; no nave
and no chancel.

The removal of idolatrous images from the Church, including statues,
also meant that the polyphonic singing of church choirs – which had
been a major feature of the abbeys and monasteries – was abandoned.
The beautiful music of the Scottish composer Robert Carver; the few
carvings that survive – even High Crosses were seen as idolatrous; and
the illuminated mistrals and books of hours which do remain, would
have been lost to posterity if the Reformers had been entirely successful
in their destruction. As it was, both Church and State co-operated to
attempt to remove all popular vestiges of pre-Reformation worship, such
as fetes and festivals.

However, human habit – or need – to continue certain traditions
conspired deliberately, or otherwise, to frustrate their attempts. Thus,
throughout the 17th century, church records tell of visits to healing wells
for cures; and the perpetuation of rites which were regarded as
papistical. Although festivals and fetes may have had religious origins,
they developed secular purposes for markets and other legal purposes,
which were equally important in day-to-day life. The practice of allowing
funerary effigies to be placed inside the church building was also halted,
although several fine examples of pre-Reformation tombs remain today.

Unrest and Upheaval – Covenant to Disruption

During the remainder of the 16th century and into the 17th, the religious
settlement in Scotland continued to cause problems, particularly during
the reigns of James VI and Charles I. In the early part of the 17th century,
James's ecclesiastical policies re-introduced certain features of
Episcopacy – the administration of the Church by bishops – which were
as much a result of his own religious convictions as lack of unity within
the Church.

At the time of the Reformation, the Church had relied on the support
of the nobles to achieve religious and political goals, but during the 1580s
to 1630s there was much criticism of some of the nobles, who were seen
as not fulfilling their role as godly magistrates. One of the main critics,
and especially critical of God's chief magistrate – the King himself – was

Andrew Melville, regarded by many as being the real force behind the introduction of the Presbyterian system. He argued vehemently against any lay interference in Church organisation.

During this period, the lack of co-operation or communication between Church and State led to stalemate. Despite the Church's rejection of the Crown's involvement in Church policy, James issued, and was able to get the General Assembly to ratify, certain acts which gradually reduced the power of the Reformers.

The *Black Act* of 1584 removed the authority of the 13 presbyteries over Church matters, although the *Golden Act* of 1592 did restore this power. But the *Five Articles of Perth* of 1618, which had initially been rejected at the General Assembly at St Andrews the previous year, re-introduced kneeling at prayer, private communion, confirmation by bishop, observance of holy days and private baptism; all of which, although an illustration of James's belief in his divine right authority, actually contributed to the eventual protest and strife of the 1630s and later.

Charles I continued his father's autocratic attitude to the Church, but this only provoked unity among his opponents. Charles's introduction of the *Common Prayer Book* in 1637 resulted in the signing of the *National Covenant* in 1638, asserting the people's right to have a Reformed Church, administered without interference from the King. The Covenant was first signed by a small group of nobles in February 1638 at Greyfriars Churchyard, in Edinburgh, and at the General Assembly of that

Greyfriars Churchyard

year, Charles's prayer book was banned along with the *Five Articles of Perth*. Charles attempted to restore his authority with the Bishop's wars of 1639 and 1640, but the outcome was mixed and a short uneasy peace followed.

Initially the Covenanters were successful, and Charles acquiesced to their demands in order to calm the situation in England and Ireland. In 1643 the *Solemn League and Covenant* – a religious and military pact between the Parliamentarians, in England, and the Covenanters, in Scotland – was signed, but was never fully accepted by the English. Charles, however, was defeated by a combined English and Scottish army at Marston Moor in 1644.

In Scotland the Marquis of Montrose led a rising for the King and defeated Covenanting armies at Tippermuir, Aberdeen, Inverlochy, Alford and Kilsyth. However, the Covenanting General, David Leslie eventually defeated Montrose at Philiphaugh in 1645. Charles surrendered to the Scots' army at Newark, but this did little to resolve the crisis.

The Covenanters and Royalists subdivided into the Engagers – who supported the King; and the anti-Engagers – those opposed to the King. The Engagers were defeated by Cromwell at Preston in 1648, and Charles was executed in 1649. The Scots rose against Cromwell, but were defeated at Dunbar in 1650, and the Cromwellian administration of Scotland attempted to reduce the power of the Covenanters.

With the restoration of Charles II in 1660 came the reintroduction of bishops in 1662. Even before this, in 1660, an act was passed banning conventicles – Covenanters meeting to worship as they pleased – as a result of fear of religious opposition. In 1666 the Covenanters rose and marched on Edinburgh, but their ill-armed troop was routed at Rullion Green in the Pentland Hills. Peace was still not achieved, and in 1679 the Covenanters rebelled again after the murder of Archbishop James Sharp. Despite an early success at Drumclog, they were defeated in 1679 at Bothwell Brig by government troops led by the Duke of Monmouth.

The most extreme group of the Covenanters, the Cameronians – who denounced the King's authority – led by James Cameron, continued the struggle until 1680, when they finally were defeated at Airds Moss and Cameron was slain. During the 1680s, the Covenanters were persecuted, many being executed by government forces, during the period now known as the *Killing Times*. The Highlands also suffered severely.

John Graham of Claverhouse, *Bonnie Dundee* or *Bloody Clavers,* was responsible for many of the killings, including two of the most famous,

A Wee Guide to Old Churches and Abbeys of Scotland

the *Wigtown Martyrs,* in 1685. Margaret Lauchleson or McLachlan and Margaret Wilson were sentenced to death because of their Cameronian beliefs. Although they were tethered to posts to be drowned by the incoming tide, they may have been rescued. There is a monument to the two women in Kirkcudbright graveyard.

Charles II died in 1685, and his brother, James VII – a Catholic – came to the throne. The Revolution of 1689, which replaced James

Memorial to the Wigtown Martyrs, Kirkcudbright

with the Protestant William of Orange and Mary, confirmed the Westminster confession, and a Presbyterian form of Church government, but there remained small groups of dissenters. Families and individuals remained loyal to the openly Catholic Stewarts or the Catholic religion itself. Much of this support withered, however, with the failure of Jacobite Risings, most notably in 1746 when the Stewarts were decisively defeated at the Battle of Culloden.

A series of secessions within the church took place during the 18th and 19th centuries, the first in 1733. These were again mainly over the relationship between Church and State: who had control over appointments of ministers – patronage. The General Assembly had decided that only elders and heritors would elect ministers, excluding the congregation. As this denied the 'democratic' principles of the Presbyterian Church, a group, led by Ebenezer Erskine, broke away, arguing for the disestablishment of the Church. Later seceders divided off – and up – over other issues, but the common feature was patronage. The Burghers, Anti-Burghers, Auld Lights, New Lights, and the Relief Church were all established as alternatives to the Church of Scotland.

The *Disruption* of 1843 was also about patronage. The *Ten Year Conflict* started in 1833 between the Evangelicals and the Moderates. The Evangelicals had passed the Chapel and Veto acts, which allowed congregations to veto unsuitable ministers appointed by the patrons or heritors. The legality of these acts was put to the test at Auchterarder, where the candidate Robert Young was rejected by the congregation. In 1843 the Chapel Act was vetoed, and the following year Thomas Chalmers, leader of the Evangelicals, dramatically left the General Assembly, followed by 474 other ministers and set up the Free Church.

The Free Church took about 40% of the membership of the Church of Scotland with it, and in its first few years attracted much popularity and money to help build new churches. However, by the 1860s the majority of the congregations were middle-class, much like the established Church. In the Highlands the Free Church remained – and remains – popular, as it supported the crofters during their disputes with landowners in the 1880s.

In the 1890s the Free Church joined with the original seceders and Relief Church to form the United Free Church. Another branch of the Free Church broke away in the 1890s to form the Free Presbyterian Church, some of whom eventually re-united in 1900 to form the Free Church of Scotland, and the United Free Church in 1929.

At the same time Catholicism re-emerged as a major force in Scotland, as large numbers of Irish immigrants settled in the 1850s. The Scottish Episcopal Church; Judaism; Temperance movements; Muslims; Sikhs; Buddhists; New-Age Celtic Christians all established themselves, to greater or lesser degree, during the 20th century.

For some, religious beliefs are a vibrant aspect of their ethnic and cultural identity, while for others religion appears to be a thing of the past, with no relevance to modern society. What cannot be denied is that religion did play an important role in Scottish history: politically, culturally and spiritually. Because religious worship has altered so much throughout Scottish history, we are left with a great variety of physical remains. From standing stones to carved crosses, simple chapels to the Gothic splendour of cathedrals and collegiate churches, Scotland has a wealth of religious sites to visit.

OLD CHURCHES, ABBEYS AND OTHER CHRISTIAN MONUMENTS OF SCOTLAND (A–Z)

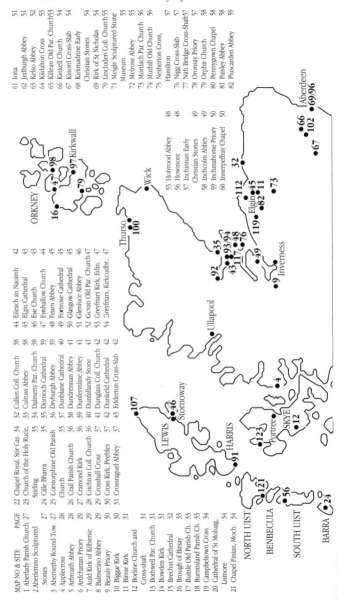

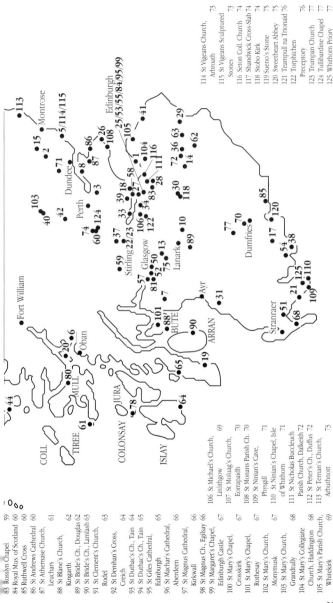

25

Key

P	Parking
S	Sales Area
☕	Refreshments
WC	Toilet
£	Admission Charge
♿	Disabled
HS	Historic Scotland
NTS	National Trust for Scotland

Numbers before entries refer to the
map on page 24-25

If a site cannot be found under its
location (eg "Leuchars" or "Rodel"),
also try under the name of the
church (eg "St Athernase"
or "St Clement's")

1 Aberlady Parish Church

NT 4622798   66

Off A198, Main Street, Aberlady, East Lothian

The body of the church was re-modelled in 1886, but the tower dates from the 16th century. The church houses an 8th-century cross, and marble monuments.

Open May to September

P Nearby S ♿ Access

2 Aberlemno Sculptured Stones

NO 523557   54   HS

Off B9134, 6 miles NE of Forfar, Angus

A magnificent cross-slab with Pictish symbols at Aberlemno, as well as other stones by the side of the B9314.

Stones covered over in winter

P Nearby

3 Abernethy Round Tower

NO 190165   58   HS

On A913, 6 miles SE of Perth

This was the site of a Culdee Celtic Christian establishment, which was refounded as a collegiate establishment in the 14th century. The slender round tower – of Irish style – was probably built by the Culdees in the 9th or 10th century, and is one of only two example in Scotland, the other being at Brechin.

Nothing remains of the collegiate church.

Open all year — key available from nearby tearoom or adjoining house

 Nearby

4 Applecross

NG 713458   24

Off A896, Applecross, 1 mile N of village, Wester Ross

Site of an early Christian community, founded in 673 by St Maelrubha, who was from Bangor in Ireland. A fine 8th-century cross-slab stands by the gate of the church, and inside the modern church there are a further three carved fragments of other slabs, found at the east end of the graveyard. While the existing church dates from 1817, the nearby ruined chapel – roofed over by greenery – was built in the 15th century.

Open all year

5 Arbroath Abbey

NO 643413   54   HS

Off A92, in Arbroath, Angus

Substantial ruins of a Tironensian abbey, founded in 1178 by William the Lyon, in memory of his friend Thomas a' Becket. Part of the church survives, including the fine west end, the gatehouse, sacristy and Abbot's House, which houses a museum. The cloister and other domestic buildings are very ruined. The Declaration of Arbroath was signed here in 1320, and the Stone of Scone was set before the high altar here after being taken from Westminster Abbey in 1951.

☎ 01241 878756—Open all year

 Nearby S   &

Medieval wood panel – Abbot's House, Arbroath Abbey

6 Ardchattan Priory

NM 971349 49 HS

Off A828 or B845, 6.5 miles NE of Oban, N shore of Loch Etive, Argyll

Ruins of a Valliscaulian priory, some of which has been incorporated into a house, founded about 1231 by Duncan MacDougall. Burnt by Cromwell's troops in 1654. Floor slabs, grave stones, and early Christian carved wheel cross survive.

Ruin open all year

 Nearby

7 Auld Kirk of Kilbirnie

NS 314546 63

Off B780, Dalry Road, Kilbirnie, Ayrshire

The Auld Kirk dates from before the Reformation, and stands on the site of a 6th-century abbey of St Brendan of Clonfert. The nave dates from 1470, and the tower from 1490. Fine Italian Renaissance style carving from 1642.

☎ 01505 683459—Open July to August weekdays 2-4pm

 Nearby S wc ♿ Access

8 Balmerino Abbey

NO 358246 59 NTS

Off A914, 4.5 miles SW of Newport on Tay, Fife

Remains of a 13th-century Cistercian Abbey in a peaceful setting, founded by Ermengarde, widow of William the Lyon, and their son, Alexander II, in 1229. Only the basement of the chapter house and adjoining buildings survive, while the church is very ruinous. Mary, Queen of Scots, had dinner at the Abbey in 1565. Interesting chestnut tree, said to have been planted by the monks.

Open all year

 Nearby

9 Beauly Priory

NH 527465   26   HS

On A862, in Beauly,
Highlands

The fine ruined cruciform
church of a Valliscaulian
priory, dedicated to St Mary
and St John the Baptist,
founded in 1230 by John
Bisset and Alexander II.
Became a Cistercian house
around 1510. There are
some old burial slabs and
tombs, one of Prior
Mackenzie. The church was
roofless by 1633, and the
cloister and domestic
buildings were demolished,
the stone said to have been
used by Cromwell to build a fort at Inverness in 1650. The north transept
was restored in 1901 as the Kintail burial aisle.

Open all year

10 Biggar Kirk

NT 042378   72

Off A72 or A702, Biggar, Lanarkshire

Impressive 16th-century church, dedicated to St Mary, with a crenellated
tower, which is still used as the parish church. The church was a
collegiate establishment, founded by Malcolm Lord Fleming in 1545,
although it probably incorporates older work. The tower has gunloops
for muskets. It was restored in 1870-1 and again in 1934-5.

Open daily in summer; in winter key available from Moat Park
Heritage Centre, opposite

 Nearby S

11 Birnie Kirk

NJ 206587   28

Off B9010, 2.5 miles S of Elgin, Moray

Standing on a kirkyard mound, Birnie Kirk dates from the 12th century, and the chancel arch, the north and south doorways and the font date from this time. The church is dedicated to St Brandon, and was altered in 1734 and 1891. Birnie was one of the places where the Bishops of Moray had a cathedral before removing to Elgin, and there is an early Pictish stone in the kirkyard.

12 Borline Church and Cross-shaft

NG 375259   32

Off B8009, Glen Eynort, Skye

In a wooded burial ground, are the ruins of two churches, the smaller being dedicated to St Maelrubha. Outside the west end of the larger church are several fine carved slabs and part of a cross-shaft. A carved font was found here in the 19th century, and is now in the Royal Museum of Scotland.

13 Bothwell Parish Church

NS 705586   64

Off A725, Main Street, Bothwell, Lanarkshire

Occupying the site of a 6th-century church, the present building has a medieval choir, although the nave and tower date from 1833. The church was a collegiate establishment, and was founded by Archibald the Grim, 3rd Earl of Douglas, in 1398, and was dedicated to St Bride. The church houses 17th- and 18th-century monuments. Graveyard.

Open daily Easter to September

 Nearby S [WC] & Access

14 Bowden Kirk

NT 554303   73

Off A699, 5 miles E of Selkirk, Bowden, Borders

Founded in 1128, part of the existing Kirk probably dates from the 15th

31

century or earlier, while most is from the 17th century. The church was
re-modelled in 1794, and again in 1909. Interesting monuments,
including burial vaults of the Dukes of Roxburghe, and memorial to Lady
Grizel Baillie. Notable tombstones in graveyard.

Open all year

P Nearby S (post office) wc & Access

15 Brechin Cathedral

NO 596601   44

Off A935, Brechin, Angus

Mostly medieval church, housing an early sculptured stone, still used as
the parish church. Much of the nave was built in the 13th century, but
was unsympathetically re-modelled in 1806, as were the aisles and west

front. Between 1900-2, the cathedral was restored to its original design.
Adjacent is an unusual 11th-century round tower, one of only two of
which survive in Scotland, the other at Abernethy.

Open all year

P Nearby S

16 Brough of Birsay

NY 239285   6   HS

Tidal island, 20 miles NW of Kirkwall, Orkney

Remains of early Celtic Christian settlement, later taken over by Norsemen. A ruinous church, consisting of a rectangular nave, smaller chancel and an apse, was built here around the beginning of the 12th century. Foundations of enclosure wall, and several other buildings remain. A sculptured stone, decorated with human and geometric designs, was discovered here, but is now in the Royal Museum of Scotland, Edinburgh.

Open all year – check tides as causeway floods

 Nearby

17 Buittle Old Parish Church

NX 807598   84

Off A745, SE of Castle Douglas, Dumfries and Galloway

Dating from 1234-96, the roofless church consists of a plain nave to which a wider, more elaborate chancel was added in the late 13th or early 14th century. The church remained in use until the nearby present parish church was built in 1819.

Open all year

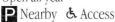 Nearby & Access

18 Burntisland Parish Church

NT 234857   66

Off A921, East Leven Street, Burntisland

This was the first post-Reformation church, built between 1590-1600, to an unusual square design, and still in use. The General Assembly met here in 1601, in the presence of James VI, when a new translation of the Bible was approved.

Open June to August 2-4pm; other times key available from tourist office or curator – ☎ 01592 873275

P Nearby S WC & Access

19 Campbeltown Cross

NR 720204   68

Off A83, NE end of Main Street, Campbeltown, Kintyre

A fine 14th-century carved cross, decorated on both sides with figures of saints including St Michael slaying the dragon, and decorative motifs. The Cross was brought here from Kilkivan in the 17th century.

Open all year

P Nearby

20 Cathedral of St Moluag, Lismore

NM 860434   49

Off B8045, 2.5 miles from Achnacroish, Lismore

The choir of the 14th-century cathedral of Argyll and the Isles survives as the parish church, while only foundations remain of the nave and tower. The choir was roofless by 1679, but was restored in 1749 at which time the walls were lowered by as much as ten feet. Several carved slabs, dating from medieval times, survive in the graveyard.

P Nearby & Access

21 Chapel Finian, Mochrum

NX 278489   82   HS

On A747, 5 miles NW of Port William, Mochrum, Galloway

Only the foundations of a small rectangular chapel survive, dating from the 10th or 11th century. It was dedicated to St Finian of Moville, who was educated at Whithorn and died around 579.

Open all year

P Nearby

22 Chapel Royal, Stirling Castle

NS 793942   57   HS

In Stirling, at Castle

The earliest reference to a chapel at Stirling Castle is in 1124. The present chapel was re-modelled by James VI in 1594, who was himself baptised here. The ceiling and part of the walls were decorated in 1628. By the early 20th century, the building was used as a school and dining hall. The restoration to return it to its 16th-century design was started in the 1930s, and the painted ceiling and walls can still be seen.

Open all year as Stirling Castle

 S WC & Access

23 Church of the Holy Rude, Stirling

NS 793937   57

Off A9, Stirling, St John Street – near Stirling Castle

A fine church, built in the 16th and 17th centuries, and used for the coronation of James VI in 1567, at which John Knox preached. The church has a medieval nave, and the choir and apse were added in 1555. Still used as parish church. Historic churchyard.

Open May to September 10am-5pm

S   WC

24 Cille Bharra

NF 704073   31

Off A888, Eoligarry, Barra

The ruined remains of a medieval church, built about the 12th century and dedicated to St Barr. Two chapels also survive, one of which has been re-roofed to provide shelter for several carved slabs from the churchyard. Other interesting slabs lie in the yard, while a fine carved stone, with a cross and runic inscription, is kept in the Royal Museum of Scotland.

Open all year

 Nearby

25 Corstorphine Old Parish Church

NT 201728   66

Off A8, Kirk Loan, Corstorphine, Edinburgh

Dating from the 14th century, the Old Parish Church has a stone-slabbed roof and a 15th-century tower, and was used as a collegiate church. Tombs contained within the church include that of the founders of the collegiate church, Sir Adam Forrester, Lord Provost of Edinburgh (died 1405), and Sir John Forrester, Lord Chamberlain during the reign of James I. The collegiate establishment was dedicated to St John the

Baptist. Interesting gravestones.

Open Wed 10.30-12 noon all year, except December and January

P Nearby S &b Limited Access

26 Crail Parish Church

NO 614080 59

On A917, Marketgate, Crail, Fife

Built in 1243, this large aisled church was altered in 1517, when it was raised to collegiate level by William Myrton. Dedicated to St Maelrubha or St Mary, the church was further altered in later centuries. Pictish cross slab inside south entrance. Interesting graveyard.

Open June to mid-September

P Nearby S WC &b Access

27 Cramond Kirk

NT 190769 66

Off A90, Cramond Glebe Road, Cramond, Edinburgh

Set in the picturesque village of Cramond. The tower dates from the 15th-century, although most of the rest of this cruciform kirk was built in 1656, and altered in following centuries. Fine roof. Interesting graveyard.

Open daily during Edinburgh Festival 2–5 pm

P Nearby S WC &b Acc

28 Crichton Collegiate Church

NT 381616 66

Off B6367, 1.5 miles E of Gorebridge, Midlothian

Substantial and impressive collegiate church, dedicated to St Mary and St Kentigern,

Crichton Collegiate Church

dating from 1449, with a square crenellated tower. Fine pointed barrel
vaults over the choir and transepts, and square tower over the crossing. It
would appear the nave was never built. The collegiate establishment was
founded by William Crichton, Lord Chancellor of Scotland – Crichton
Castle is a short walk away.

Open May to September Sun 2–5 pm

  Access

29 Crosshall Cross

NT 760422 74

On B6461, 0.5 miles N of Eccles, Crosshall, Borders

The cross, about 10 feet high, is carved on all four sides, and dates from
medieval times. It has a round head, and decorative features include
crosses, a rough figure and a hound.

Open all year

 Nearby & Access

30 Cross Kirk, Peebles

NS 250407 73 HS

Off A72, in Peebles, Borders

The ruins of Trinitarian Friary, founded about 1474, and named after the
discovery of a large cross and inscribed stone on the site in 1261. It was
dedicated to St Nicholas, and was a place of pilgrimage. The church was
taken over by the parish in 1561, and used until 1784, after which the
buildings became ruinous. Much of the late 13th-century church survives,
however, consisting of the nave, chancel and sacristy, with later burial
aisles.

Open all year

31 Crossraguel Abbey

NS 275083 76 HS

On A77, 2 miles S of Maybole, Ayrshire

Substantial and well-preserved ruin of a Cluniac abbey, founded by
Duncan, Earl of Carrick in 1216. The original church was cruciform, but
after damage during the Wars of Independence with England in 1306, the

monastic buildings were rebuilt and the church lost its transepts. A well-preserved gatehouse, cloister and abbot's house, with an adjoining 16th-century tower house, also survive. The Abbey was dissolved during the Reformation, although there were monks here until 1592. Exhibition.

☎ 01655 883113—Open daily April to September except closed Thur PM and Fri

32 Cullen Collegiate Church

NJ 507663   29

Off A98, 0.75 miles SW of Cullen town centre

A fine well-preserved collegiate church, founded in 1543 by Alexander Ogilvie, and dedicated to St Mary. Still used as the parish church, the building is of cruciform plan: the nave dates from the 13th century, the south transept from 1536, and the north transept from the 18th century. The church houses a 16th-century carved grave slab and a stone effigy of Alexander Ogilvie of Deskford, who died in 1554.

Open all year – if closed, key obtainable at the Manse, Seafield Place

33 Culross Abbey

NS 989863   65   HS

Off B9037, Kirk Street, Culross

Situated in the pretty town of Culross. A Cistercian abbey, dedicated to St Serf and St Mary, was founded here in 1217 by Malcolm, Earl of Fife on the site of a Celtic Christian establishment. The abbey was dissolved during the Reformation and most of the buildings are ruinous, except for the monk's choir, used as the parish church since 1633. The remains of the domestic buildings are open to the public.

Open all year

 Access

34 Dalmeny Parish Church

NT 144775   65

Off B924, Dalmeny, Lothian

A fine and largely unaltered medieval Romanesque church, founded in the 12th century, dedicated to St Cuthbert. Fine south doorway, the arch stones carved with animals, figures and grotesque heads. Historic graveyard.

Open April to September, Sun 2–4.30 pm. Key available from manse or post office – ☎ 0131 331 1479

P Nearby S WC ♿ Access

35 Dornoch Cathedral

NH 797896 21

Off A949, Castle Street, Dornoch

Although restored in the 19th century, much of the 13th-century cruciform-plan cathedral of the Bishops of Caithness survives, including the chancel and crossing piers. It was founded in 1223 by Gilbert de Moravia, Bishop of Caithness from 1223-46. The nave was destroyed by fire in 1570 after being torched by the Mackays of Strathnaver, and the transepts and choir were not re-roofed until 1616. The nave was rebuilt and the rest of the building restored in the 19th century. Opposite the cathedral is part of the bishop's palace, a tall tower house, now used as a hotel.

Open all year

P Nearby S ♿ Access

36 Dryburgh Abbey

NT 591316 74 HS

Off B6356, Dryburgh, 5 miles SE of Melrose, Borders

A picturesque and substantial ruin, Dryburgh Abbey dates from the 12th and 13th centuries, and is where

Dryburgh Abbey

Sir Walter Scott is buried. It was founded by David I, and was a Premonstratensian establishment, dedicated to St Mary. Part of the church survives, as do substantial portions of the cloister, including the fine chapter house, parlour and vestry. The Abbey was sacked by the English in 1322, 1385 and 1545, and was dissolved in 1587. The buildings continued to be lived in by the secular owners, the Erskines, until 1671.

☎ 01835 822381—Open all year

P S ♿ ⅙ ♿ Access

37 Dunblane Cathedral

NN 782015   57   HS

Off B8033, in Dunblane, Stirlingshire

In the picturesque town of Dunblane, by the banks of the Allen river. Although there was probably a church here from early Christian times, the Cathedral is substantially 13th century, except for the bell tower, which is earlier. The Cathedral became ruinous after the Reformation, except for the choir, but the whole building has been restored. Fine carving within the church, medieval stalls survive, and there is a 9th-century cross slab. Still used as the parish church.

Dunblane Cathedral – wood carving

☎ 01786 823338—Open all year

P Nearby S ♿ ⅙ Access

38 Dundrennan Abbey

NX 749475   83   HS

On A711, Dundrennan, 5 miles SE of Kirkcudbright, Dumfries and Galloway

The ruins of a Cistercian abbey founded in 1142 by David I and dedicated to the Blessed Virgin Mary. Substantial parts of the church, chapter house and cloister survive. The Abbey was dissolved during the Reformation, although the last Abbot died in 1605, and part of the church was used by the parish until 1742. By then most of the domestic buildings had been demolished, and much of the church was also destroyed at this time.

☎ 01557 500262—Open April to September

 S &

39 Dunfermline Abbey

NT 089873   65   HS

Off A907 or A823, in Dunfermline, Fife

Remains of a substantial 11th-century Benedictine abbey, founded by Queen Margaret. Original foundations are under the 12th-century Romanesque nave. The choir, which is now the present parish church, is where Robert the Bruce, Robert I, is buried, as well as many others of the Scottish royalty. Substantial ruins remain of some of the domestic buildings, including the refectory and the royal palace. Exhibition.

☎ 01383 739026—Choir closed October to March

 Nearby S &

40 Dunfallandy Stone

NN 946564   53   HS

Off A9, 1 mile S of Pitlochry, Perthshire

A fine Pictish sculptured cross-slab, dating from the 9th century, with a cross surrounded by various animals, beasts and angels.

Open all year

 Nearby

41 Dunglass Collegiate Church

NT 766718 67 HS

Off A1, Dunglass, 1 mile NW of Cockburnspath, East Lothian

Ruined but fine cross-shaped church of St Mary, founded about 1450 as a college of canons, by Sir Alexander Home. It has a stone-vaulted ceiling, central tower, and stone-slabbed roof. The church was held against English raiders in 1544, but by the 18th century was being used as a barn.

Open all year

P Nearby

42 Dunkeld Cathedral

N0 025426 53 HS

Off A923, Dunkeld, Perthshire

Standing in a picturesque setting in Dunkeld on the banks of the Tay. The 14th-century choir is used as the parish church, although the nave is ruined. Chapter house has a small museum. The tower, ruined nave and south porch in the care of Historic Scotland.

Open all year

P Nearby S WC & Access

43 Edderton Cross-Slab

NH 719842 21

Off A9, 0.5 miles E of cross-roads at Edderton, Ross and Cromarty

Standing in the graveyard of the 18th-century church is a carved cross-slab. On one side is a cross below which is a rider within a curved frame, while on the other side is a large ringed cross on a tall stem. There are the remains of an earlier church to the east of the modern building.

Open all year

P Nearby & Access

44 Eileach an Naoimh

NM 640097 55 HS

An island in the Garvellach group, north of Jura.

The ruins of beehive cells from an early Christian community, a medieval chapel and graveyard stand on this remote island. Other features of early date include a small underground cell and the traditional burial place of

Eithne, Columba's mother. The island can be reached from
Toberonochy, Luing, by hired boat, subject to weather conditions.
Open all year—see above

45 Elgin Cathedral

NJ 222632   28   HS
Off A96, Elgin, Moray
Substantial ruined
cathedral, once one of the
most impressive churches
in Scotland, dating from
the 13th century. It was
founded in 1224 as the seat
of the Bishops of Moray,
after they removed from
Spynie. The Cathedral was
torched by Alexander
Stewart, the Wolf of
Badenoch, in 1390,
because the Bishop had
excommunicated him for
deserting his wife. The
church was rebuilt, but

after the Reformation decayed quickly, the central tower collapsing in
1711 and bringing down most of the nave and transepts. Fine chapter
house. Pictish cross-slab, stone effigy of a bishop, and fine table tombs.
Exhibition. Interesting graveyard.

  The Bishop's Palace, at Spynie, is also open to the public – although it is
more of a castle than a palace.

☎ 01343 547171—Open all year – joint entry ticket Spynie Palace
🅿 Nearby   S   ⅏

46 Eye Church

NB 484322   8
Off A866, Aignish, Lewis
Said to be built on the site of the cell of St Catan, a contemporary of St
Columba, the existing rectangular ruined church dates from medieval

Eye Church

times. The burial place of the MacLeods of Lewis, there are two carved stones within the church: one depicts a warrior and is believed to be Roderick, 7th Chief; while the other is for Margaret, daughter of Roderick MacLeod of Lewis, who died in 1503.

Open all year

 Nearby

47 Eynhallow Church

HY 359288   6

On S side of island of Eynhallow, Orkney

The existing building, dating from the 12th century, was probably once part of a monastic establishment. The church consisted of a rectangular nave with a porch at one end and a square-ended chancel. However, the building was re-modelled in the 16th-century to make it a dwelling, and its older original was not revealed until 1854.

Open all year

48 Fearn Abbey

NH 837773 21

Off B9166, Fearn, Highland

Known as the 'Lamp of the North', this 14th-century church is one of the oldest pre-Reformation Scottish churches still used for worship. The Abbey was a Premonstratensian establishment of the Order of St Augustine, founded by Ferquhard Macintaggart, Earl of Ross, around 1227. The Abbey church was rebuilt in 1772 – after the nave roof had collapsed in 1742 killing 44 people – and in 1972, but little remains of the other abbey buildings. Patrick Hamilton, Commendator of the abbey from 1517, was burnt for heresy at St Andrews in 1528.

Open May to September Sat and Sun 10am-4.30pm

 S &. Access

49 Fortrose Cathedral

NH 727565 27 HS

Off A832, Fortrose, Highland

Only the south aisle and the undercroft of the chapter house survive from the medieval cathedral of Ross, but the plan of the buildings are laid out in the grass. Bishop Robert moved here from Rosemarkle between 1214-49 and built the cathedral. The cathedral was a long rectangle, with buttressed walls and a tower. Within the aisles are three arched tombs: Euphemia, Countess of Ross, who was forced to marry Alexander Stewart, the Wolf of Badenoch; Bishop Cairncross, who died in 1545; and Bishop Fraser, who died in 1507.

Open all year

50 Glasgow Cathedral

NS 602655 64 HS

Centre of Glasgow

Dedicated to St Mungo, the present cruciform church with a central tower, is the only medieval cathedral in mainland Scotland to have survived the Reformation complete. The present church, dating from the 13th century, was built over the tomb of St Mungo or Kentigern, although there was probably a church here from the 6th century. Bishop Blackadder started the incomplete Blackadder Aisle on the south side of the church in the 15th century, and the west end of the church was flanked by two towers, which were demolished in 1846. The building has a fine crypt, and a 15th-century stone screen.

☎ 0141 552 6891—Open all year

P Nearby ☕ S 🚾 ♿ Access

51 Glenluce Abbey

NX 185586 82 HS

Off A75, 1.5 miles N of Glenluce village, Dumfries and Galloway

Ruins of a Cistercian abbey of the Blessed Virgin Mary, dating from 1192,

and founded by Roland, Lord of Galloway. Not much remains of the church, but the fine 16th-century chapter house is still roofed and parts of the cloister buildings survive. Exhibition.

☎ 01581 300541—Open daily April to September; weekends only October to March

P S ⚓ ♿ Access

52 Govan Old Parish Church

NS 553658   64   HS

Off A739, 866 Govan Road, Govan, Glasgow

The present church, dedicated to St Constantine and dating from 1888, was built on the site of a much older establishment and is surrounded by an interesting graveyard. The church houses a fine collection of early Christian stones, including a decorated sarcophagus, five hogback tombstones, two cross-shafts and upright crosses, and a number of recumbent slabs.

☏ 0141 445 1941—Open by arrangement only

P Nearby S [wc]

53 Greyfriars Kirk, Edinburgh

NT 258734   66

Greyfriars Place, Edinburgh

Built on the site of a Franciscan Friary – hence the name 'Greyfriars' – this was the first post-Reformation church built in Edinburgh, and was completed in 1620. It was altered in following centuries. The National Covenant was signed here in 1638. Historic kirkyard – formerly the garden of the Friary – with 16th-century monuments, Covenanters' prison and memorial to Greyfriars Bobby.

Open April to October Mon to Fri 10.30-4.30pm; Sat 10.30-2.30pm; November to March Thu 1.30-3.30pm; Kirkyard open all year

P Nearby S [wc] ♿ Access

54 Greyfriars, Kirkcudbright

NX 683511   84

Off A711, Kirkcudbright, Dumfriesshire

A Franciscan friary was founded here in 1455 by James II, although the remains of the present church may date from the 13th century. Part of the building was re-modelled in 1730, fell into disuse, then became part of a school. The church was restored in 1922.

Open all year

P Nearby

55 Holyrood Abbey

NT 269740 66 HS

Edinburgh, in the grounds of Holyroodhouse

The ruined church of an Augustinian abbey of the Holy Cross, founded by David I in 1128, survives beside Holyrood Palace. The Abbey was sacked by the English in 1322, 1385, 1544 and in 1547. The east end of the church was demolished during the Reformation, and the nave – the surviving portion – became the parish church. In 1672 it was made a Chapel Royal, but it was ransacked by an angry mob in 1688. The roof collapsed in 1768. The most impressive part is the west facade, and one aisle is still roofed.

The Palace was developed out of the guest house of the Abbey as a more comfortable alternative to Edinburgh Castle, and was enlarged in following centuries, occupying part of the former cloister, and is still the residence of the monarch in Scotland.

☎ 0131 556 1096—Open all year except when royal family in residence

🅿 Nearby S ⅃

56 Howmore Church and Chapels

NF 758365 22

Off 865, Tobha Mor, N of Howmore village, South Uist

The complex at Howmore, once surrounded by marshes and with plenty of mud still around, consists of the ruined remains of two churches and two chapels, while a third was demolished in 1866. The largest of buildings 'Teampull Mor' – St Mary's or the Large Church – may date from the 13th century and was used as the parish church, although not much now remains. The other buildings, all ruined, on the site are Dugall's Chapel; St Dermot's Chapel, with an early Christian cross-marked grave slab; and Clan Ranald's Chapel. By the 16th century, Howmore was the burial site for Clan Ranald, who had held South Uist since the 1370s.

Open all year

 Nearby

57 Inchinnan Early Christian Stones

NS 479689   64

Off A8, Inchinnan, Renfrew

Three sculptured stones lie in a covered area between the church and bell-tower, and consist of a carved sarcophagus, grave-slab and cross-shaft. Inchinnan was an early Christian community, dedicated to St Conval, an Irish saint. The present church was built when the old medieval church was demolished to make way for Glasgow Airport.

Open all year

  &. Access

58 Inchcolm Abbey

NT 191827   66   HS

On a picturesque island in the Firth of Forth

Very well preserved group of monastic buildings, founded in 1123 by Alexander I and dedicated to St Columba. Alexander had been crossing the Forth at Queensferry but his ship was engulfed by a storm. He was washed up on Inchcolm and was helped by a hermit on the island.

  The English sacked the Abbey in 1542 and 1547, and in 1548 it was occupied by English, then French, garrisons. The last Mass said here was in 1560.

  The cloister and chapter house are complete, and many of the other buildings are in a good state of preservation. The island was used as a quarantine station, fort, Russian naval hospital, and had gun emplacements built to defend the Forth Bridge. Exhibition.

☎ 01383 823332—Closed in winter – ferry from South Queensferry or North Queensferry (☎ 0131 331 4857)

S WC &.

Inchmahome Priory

59 Inchmahome Priory

NN 574005 57 HS

Off A81, island in the Lake of Menteith, Stirlingshire

Picturesque ruins of a small Augustinian priory, dedicated to St Colman, on a lovely wooded island. The priory was founded in 1238 by Walter Comyn, 4th Earl of Menteith, although there may have been an earlier Christian community on the island. Robert Bruce visited the priory, and David II was married here. Mary Queen of Scots was sent here for safety in 1547 before leaving for France via Dumbarton. The chapter house is still roofed, and a substantial part of the church also survives.

☎ 01877 385294—Open April to September – parking and ferry from Port of Menteith

 S ᵂᶜ ♿

60 Innerpeffray Chapel

NN 902183 58 HS

Off B8062, 4 miles S of Crieff, Innerpeffray, Perthshire

A low rectangular collegiate church, founded by Lord Drummond about 1508 and dedicated to the Blessed Virgin Mary, although there had been a church here from 1342 or earlier. It retains the altar and other furnishings, and at one end has the Laird's Loft, above the church, reached by a spiral staircase. The adjoining building houses a library founded in 1691 by David, 3rd Lord Madderty, one of the oldest public libraries in

Scotland.

Open all year except Sun and Thu

 (£ library)

61 Iona Abbey & Nunnery

NM 287245 48

Off A849, Island of Iona, Argyll

Situated on the beautiful and peaceful island of Iona. St Columba came here from Ireland in 563, formed a monastic community, and converted the Picts on the mainland to Christianity. He died in 597, and St Columba's shrine, within the abbey buildings, dates from the 9th century. The abbey was abandoned after Viking raids of the early 9th century, but was re-established by Queen Margaret in the 11th century. Some of the surviving abbey buildings date from early 13th century after it had been refounded as a Benedictine establishment by Reginald, son of Somerled, Lord of the Isles. The Abbey was used as the cathedral of the Bishop of the Isles in the 16th century.

Although the buildings became very ruined after the Reformation, the abbey church and cloister were rebuilt in 1938 for the Iona Community.

St Martin's Cross and St John's Cross – the latter a replica – stand just outside the abbey church, and the museum houses splendid sculptured stones and crosses, one of the largest collections of early Christian carved stones in Europe. Between the abbey and nunnery (see below) is MacLean's Cross, a fine 15th-century carved stone cross.

Many of the early Kings of Scots are buried in *Reilig Odhrain* – the 'Street of the Dead' – as well as kings of Ireland and Norway. The 12th-century chapel of St Oran also survives.

The nearby Augustinian nunnery of St Mary was founded in 1208, also by Reginald, and is a fine consolidated ruin.

Open all year – parking and ferry (£) from Fionnphort, no cars on Iona

 S ꃬ ꝸ Limited

62 Jedburgh Abbey

NT 650204 74 HS

Off A68, Jedburgh, Borders

Founded by David I about 1138 as an Augustinian abbey, much of the impressive Romanesque and early Gothic church and some foundations of the domestic buildings survive. The Abbey was sacked numerous times by the English, and after an attack in 1544-5 the ruined monastic buildings were used as a quarry. The church was used by the parish until 1875 when the crown arch and vaulting of the crossing collapsed, and although unroofed, is in a good state of preservation. Visitor centre.

☎ 01835 863925—

Jedburgh Abbey

Open all year

P Nearby ☕ S 🚻 ♨ ♿ 🚻/Limited access

63 Kelso Abbey

NT 729338 74 HS

Off 698, Kelso, Borders

This was one of the richest and largest monastic establishments in Scotland, yet it is much more ruinous than the other Border abbeys. It was originally founded as a Tironensian abbey of the Blessed Virgin and St John in 1113 at Selkirk, but was moved here in 1138. Much of the church and abbey was destroyed by the English in 1544-5, although the establishment was not dissolved until 1560. The west transept was used as the parish church, and little else now remains.

Open all year

P Nearby ♿ Limited access

64 Kildalton Cross and Chapel

NR 458508   60   HS

Off A846, 7 miles NE of
Port Ellen, on Islay

The finest surviving intact
High Cross in Scotland,
dating from the 8th century,
and carved from a single slab.
This ringed cross has a
representation of the Virgin
and Child flanked by angels
on one side, while the other
has serpent and boss patterns
with four lions around the
central boss. Other represen-
tations illustrate biblical
scenes.

The small ruined chapel,
dedicated to St John the
Beloved, dates from the 12th
or 13th century, and is a
simple rectangular building. It houses many carved grave slabs, and there
are more in the churchyard. The 15th-century Thief's Cross is nearby.

Open all year

P Nearby

65 Killean Old Parish Church

NR 695445   62

Off A83, Killean, Kintyre

Dedicated to St John, the ruined church has a 12th-century nave, 13th-
century chancel, and a 15th-century north aisle, and is now the burial
aisle of the MacDonalds of Largie. It was abandoned in 1770. An early
Christian cross from the site is now in the Campbeltown museum, but
there are several fine carved slabs in the church and churchyard.

Open all year

P Nearby   ♿ Limited Access

66 Kinkell Church

NJ 785190   38   HS

Off A96 and B993, 2 miles S of Inverurie, Kinkell

The ruins remain of a 16th-century church, dedicated to St Michael.
There is a fine sacrament house of 1524; and the richly carved grave slab
of Gilbert de Greenlaw, killed at the Battle of Harlaw in 1411.

Open all year

P Nearby ♿ Limited Access

67 Kinord Cross-Slab

NO 440997   37

Off B9119, 3 miles W of Aboyne, Kinord, Aberdeenshire

This is a fine cross-slab, dating from the 9th century. The cross is filled
with interlaced knotwork.

Open all year

P Nearby ♿ Limited Access

68 Kirkmadrine Early Christian Stones

NX 080483   82   HS

Off A716, S of Sandhead, Kirkmadrine, Galloway

Displayed in the porch of the 19th-century chapel are the oldest Christian
monuments in Scotland outside Whithorn. A pillar stone, dating from the
5th century, is carved with a circled cross and Latin inscription *Here lie
the holy and chief priests, Ides, Viventius and Mavorius*. The two other
5th-century stones are also inscribed.

Open all year

P Nearby ♿ Access

69 Kirk of St Nicholas

NJ 931064   38

Off A92, Back Wynd, Aberdeen

Dating from the 12th century, the present church – the *Mither Kirk* of
Aberdeen – was largely rebuilt in the 18th and 19th centuries, but retains
the vaulted 15th-century St Mary's Chapel. Interesting monuments,
including 17th-century embroidered wall hangings.

Open May to September Mon to Sat PM

P Nearby S wc ♿ Access

70 Lincluden Collegiate Church

NX 965779   84   HS

Off A76, 1.25 miles N of Dumfries, Lincluden, Dumfriesshire

Although a nunnery was founded here by Uchtred, son of Fergus, Lord of
Galloway, most of the present ruins date from the 15th century, after it
had been converted to a collegiate establishment by Archibald the Grim,
3rd Earl of Douglas, in 1389. The nunnery had apparently fallen into a
place of disrepute, disgrace and disrepair. The recessed tomb and effigy
of Margaret, eldest daughter of Robert III and widow of Archibald, 4th
Earl of Douglas, survives in the north side of the choir. The college was
dissolved during the Reformation, and the buildings used as a quarry in
the 17th century. Much of the chancel and south transept survive, as
does the north range.

Open all year

 Nearby   & Access

71 Meigle Sculptured Stone Museum

NO 287447   53   HS

On A94, Meigle, Angus

A collection of 25 sculptured stones, one of the best collections of early
Christian and Dark Age sculpture in Western Europe. Exhibition.

📞 01828 640612—Open April to September

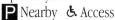

72 Melrose Abbey

NT 548341   73   HS

Off A6091, Melrose, Borders

An elegant and picturesque ruin, Melrose Abbey was founded as a
Cistercian house by David I about 1136, and was dedicated to the Blessed
Virgin Mary. The church is particularly well preserved, while the domestic
buildings and cloister are very ruinous. The Abbey suffered in the wars
with the English and was sacked in 1322, 1385 and in 1545, after which it
never recovered. It was dissolved at the Reformation, although the nave
of the church was vaulted and used as a parish church from 1618 until
1810, when it was finally abandoned.

 The heart of Robert the Bruce is buried in the nave, and many of the

powerful Douglas family are also interred here. Museum in the Abbot's house. Audio guide available. Exhibition.
☎ 01896 822562—
Open all year
 S

73 Mortlach Parish Church

NJ 323392 28
Off A941, Dufftown, Moray

The present church, dedicated to St Moluag, dates from the 13th century, but stands on the site of an early Christian site. The

Melrose Abbey – see above

chancel survives from this period, although the church was re-modelled and restored in 1826, 1876 and 1931. In one wall is the stone effigy and tomb of Alexander Leslie of Kininvie, who died about 1549; and the Battle Stone, a Pictish symbol stone, survives in the interesting graveyard.
 Nearby

74 Muthill Old Church and Tower

NN 869170 58
Off A822, 3 miles S of Crieff, Muthill

The ruinous remains of a mostly 15th-century church, consisting of an aisled nave and a tall Romanesque tower, built in the 12th or 13th century. The church was altered after the Reformation, when the chancel was abandoned and completely demolished.
 Nearby

75 Netherton Cross, Hamilton

NS 723555   64

Off A724, Strathmore Road, Hamilton Old Parish Church,
Hamilton

Standing in the graveyard is the Netherton Cross, a 10th-century
sculptured cross, decorated with figures, animals and cross-weave; as well
as Covenanting memorials. The present church was designed and built by
William Adam in 1732-4.

Church open Mon to Fri 10.30am-3.30pm

P Nearby S [WC] ᶜ Access

76 Nigg Cross-Slab

NS H 804717   21

Off B9175, Nigg, Ross and Cromarty

Housed inside Nigg Church, the fine carved cross-slab dates from the 8th
or 9th century. One side is decorated with a large cross, filled with
interlaced patterns, while the surround has elaborate boss patterns. The
other side has been badly damaged, but there are traces of figures and
animals.

P Nearby Q Lim Access

77 Nith Bridge Cross-Shaft

NX 868954   78

Off A702, Thornhill, Dumfriesshire

The most complete Anglian cross apart from Ruthwell, the Nith Bridge
Cross stands to about a height of nine feet, and carvings include animals
and winged beasts.

P Nearby

78 Oronsay Priory

NR 349889   61

Oronsay, a tidal island off Colonsay

The priory was founded in the 14th-century by John, Lord of the Isles,
and was a house of Augustinian canons. Substantial parts of the church,
cloister and domestic buildings survive. The Oronsay Cross is a fine late-
medieval carved cross. On the front is a figure of Christ being crucified

with a pattern of foliage covering both sides. There are over 30 fine carved grave slabs preserved in the Prior's House.

Open all year — on tidal island and access by foot or post-bus is regulated by tides: check locally

79 Orphir Church
HY 334044   6   HS

Off A964, 8 miles SW of Kirkwall, Orkney

The ruined remains of the only surviving round church in Scotland, dating from the 12th century. The apse survives but the rest was demolished for building a later church, itself now gone. The church was dedicated to St Nicholas, and was probably started by Earl Haakon Paulsson before 1122, whose hall – bu – was nearby.

Open all year

80 Pennygown Chapel
NM 604432   49

Off A849, Pennygown, Mull

The shell of a 13th-century chapel has the base of cross-shaft within the walls. Interesting graveyard.

Open all year

81 Paisley Abbey
NS 486640   64

Off A737, Paisley, Renfrewshire

Founded in 1163 by Walter, son of Alan, Steward of Scotland, a Cluniac priory replaced an earlier Christian community, and was dedicated to St Mirren. It became an abbey in 1219. The present church dates mostly from the 14th century, although it was rebuilt and restored in the 20th century. The church houses the effigy of Marjorie, daughter of Robert the Bruce; and the tomb of Robert II. The Barochan Cross, dating from as early as the 8th century, sculptured with warriors and human figures, is also housed here. The abbey is now used as a parish church.

☎ 0141 889 7654 Open all year – Mon to Sat 10am-3.30pm

P Nearby ☕ S WC ♿ Limited Access

82 Pluscarden Abbey

NJ 142576   28

Off B9010, 6 miles SW of Elgin, Moray

Originally founded by Alexander II in 1230, the abbey was one of only
three Valliscaulian priories in Scotland, and was dedicated to St Mary, St

John the Baptist, and St Andrew. In 1454 it became a Benedictine house,
but the church and domestic buildings became ruinous after the
Reformation. The abbey was refounded and almost completely rebuilt in
1948 as a Benedictine monastery, and there are now about 30 monks,
priests and novices.

Open all year—short walk

P Nearby S WC ⅄ Access

83 Rosslyn Chapel

NT 275631   66

Off A701, Roslin, 6 miles S of Edinburgh, Midlothian

Richly carved but partly completed – only the choir and parts of the
transept were finished – Rosslyn Chapel was founded in 1446 as a
Collegiate Church by Sir William Sinclair, and has a fine sculptured pillar,

the Prentice Pillar. It is dedicated to St Matthew, and many of the Sinclair Earls of Roslin are buried here. The roof is vaulted, and there are a mass of flying buttresses to carry the weight.

☏ 0131 440 2159—Open April to October; check winter opening

P Nearby ☕ S wc ⚐ ♿ Access

84 Royal Museum of Scotland

NT 255743 66

Queen Street, Edinburgh

The museum has material from prehistoric times to the present day, and the collections contain some of the most important items in the UK, housing many of the original artefacts found in Scotland, including the Monymusk Reliquary and St Fillan's crosier. The National Portrait Gallery is in the same building. Collections may be moved with the opening of the extension to the Chamber Street site, due to open September 1997.

☏ 0131 225 7534 —Open all year except Christmas and New Year

P Nearby ☕ S wc ♿ Access/wc

85 Ruthwell Cross

NY 100682 85 HS

Off B724, 8.5 miles SE of Dumfries, at Ruthwell

A magnificent sculptured cross, dating from the 7th century, standing about 17-feet high. It had been destroyed by order of the General Assembly in 1640, but has been reassembled from the smashed pieces. All four sides are decorated, the two wider sides with biblical scenes, while the other sides are carved with foliage and beasts.

Open all year – sited within the Parish church, key available from nearby house

P

86 St Andrews Cathedral

NO 516166 59 HS

Off A91, St Andrews, Fife

The very ruined remains of the largest cathedral in Scotland, and the adjoining Augustinian priory founded in 1144 by Robert, Bishop of St Andrews. The priory wall is well preserved.

St Regulus, or Rule, is said to have founded a monastery here in the 8th century. The relics of St Andrew were brought here in 733 by the Acca, Abbot of Hexham. The Bishopric was transferred from Abernethy in 908, and in the 12th century the Augustinian Order gradually displaced the Celtic monks. The church of the time – the tower of which, St Rule's Tower, dating from as early as 1070, survives – was too small so a large new cathedral was begun. It was at one time the longest in Britain, apart from Norwich. The building was consecrated in 1318, but had to be rebuilt after a fire in 1380. After the Reformation, the buildings fell into disuse and were demolished.

The museum houses a large collection of early Christian and medieval sculpture, including cross-slabs, effigies and other relics. St Rule's Tower is open to the public – magnificent views from top. The castle is nearby.
☎ 01334 472563—Open all year; combined ticket available for cathedral and castle
P Nearby S ♿

87 St Athernase Church, Leuchars

NO 455215 59
*Off A919,
Leuchars, Fife*
One of the finest
Norman churches in
Scotland, the
chancel and apse
with blind arcades
survive from a 12th-
century church. The
belfry was added
around 1700, and
the nave restored in
1858.

Open March to
October 9.30am-
6pm
P Nearby S [wc]

St Blane's Church, Kingarth

88 St Blane's Church, Kingarth

NS 094535   63   HS

Off A844, 2 miles S of Kingarth, south of Isle of Bute

In a peaceful and pleasant location. Site of Celtic community of the 6th century, founded by St Blane, who was born on Bute. The site is surrounded by an enclosure wall, and there are several ruined buildings, including 'The Cauldron' the purpose of which is unclear. In the middle of the site is the 12th-century chapel, with finely decorated chancel arch. There is also a upper and lower burial yard with some fine gravestones, the upper yard apparently being used for men, while the lower was for women.

Open all year – involves short walk

🅿 Nearby

89 St Bride's Church, Douglas

NS 835309   72   HS

Off A70, Main Street, Douglas

Although there was probably a church here from early times, the present fragmentary ruin probably dates from 1330 and later. The remains consist of the chancel, now roofed but open to the elements until the mid-19th century, and the remains of the south transept. The church houses the effigy of the Good Sir James, Sir James Douglas, who died in 1331 at Granada in Spain taking Bruce's heart on a pilgrimage. Other memorials are to Archibald Douglas, 5th Earl of Douglas, died 1438; and James, 7th Earl, died 1431, and his wife Beatrice Sinclair.

Open all year – instructions for obtaining the key on notice on gate

 Nearby

90 St Bride's Church, Lamlash

NS 033323 69

Off A841, N of Lamlash village, Arran

The church of St Bride, dating from the 14th-century, is now a shell, but several sculptured stones are built into the walls and lie in the graveyard. One is thought to be the grave of James Hamilton, 3rd Earl of Arran, who died in 1609.

Open all year

 Nearby

91 St Clement's Church

NG 047833 18 HS

On A859, Rodel, south of Isle of Harris, Western Isles

Fine 16th-century cruciform-plan church with a strong square tower at one end. Housed in the church is the splendid carved tomb of Alasdair Crotach MacLeod, built in 1528, although he did not die for another 20 years. The carvings include the effigy of a man in full armour, surrounded by panels of saints and other decoration,

particularly a galley, a castle, and a hunting scene. There is another tomb nearby, which is also the effigy of an armoured man. In the churchyard are several carved slabs. There is also a Shiela na Gig on the outside of the south wall of the tower.

Open all year

 Nearby

92 St Demhan's Cross, Creich

NH 636892   21

Off A9, 3 miles E of Bonar Bridge, Creich, in field E of graveyard, Sutherland

A tall carved stone, dating from the 9th or 10th century, with the outline of a large cross. The Cross is named after St Devenic. Nearby are the ruins of an 18th-century parish church, built on the site of the medieval church of St Devenic or Demhan.

Open all year

P Nearby

93 St Duthac's Church, Tain

NH 780821   21

On B9174, near the sea, Tain, Ross and Cromarty

The ruins of a medieval church, dating from the 13th century and dedicated to St Duthac, whose relics were kept here. It was from near here that Elizabeth, Queen of Robert the Bruce, and other of his

womenfolk were captured by the Earl of Ross in 1306. Despite being in an area of sanctuary, they were given into the hands of Edward I of England. The church was burnt in 1429 in the course of a feud, but was restored. James IV visited here often, as did James V, as Tain was a place of pilgrimage in medieval times.

Open all year

P Nearby

94 St Duthac's Church, Tain

NH 780821 21

On B9174, High Street, Tain, Ross and Cromarty

A well-preserved medieval church, dating from the 14th and 15th centuries and dedicated to St Duthac, a saint said to have been born in Tain about 1000. The church has large windows with restored tracery, but the interior has been stripped of most of its furnishings. A statue on the outside of the west wall is thought to be of St Duthac, and strangely survived the Reformation. The church became collegiate in 1487, founded by Thomas Hay, Bishop of Ross, who used the choir of the church, while the townsfolk used the nave. The church survived the Reformation, but around 1815 fell into disrepair after a new parish church was built, although it was restored and re-roofed in 1877.

There is also a visitor centre associated with the story of St Duthac and Tain near this church.

Open all year

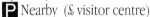 Nearby (& visitor centre)

95 St Giles Cathedral

NT 257735 66

High Street, Edinburgh

Although there has been a church here since 854, the existing complex building dates substantially from the 15th century, after the church had been sacked by the English in 1385. It has an unusual crown steeple, added in 1495. Collegiate status was granted in 1466-9, and it contained a bishop's throne from 1633-9 and 1662-90, although it was only a cathedral for a short time. The building was restored in 1829-33, when many original features were lost, and again more sympathetically in 1872-83. There are several aisles which house separate chapels and numerous war memorials.

Open all year

 Nearby ☕ S 🚾 ♿ Access

96 St Machar's Cathedral

NJ 939088 38

Off A956, Old Aberdeen, N of Aberdeen

The medieval cathedral of the Bishops of Aberdeen. The church dates mostly from the 15th century, although only half of it remains as the central tower collapsed in 1688 and the transepts are ruined. The nave and towers of the west end which survive, give some indication of the size and strength of the church at its heyday, and are now used as the parish church. The aisled church has a fine painted ceiling, completed early in the 16th century and decorated with the coats of arms of many noble families. Interesting monuments in graveyard, including the tomb of Bishop Dunbar, who died in 1533 and commissioned the ceiling, and Bishop Lichton, who had the west front built between 1422-40.

Open all year

P Nearby S ⓦⒸ ♿ Access

97 St Magnus Cathedral, Kirkwall

HY 449112 6

Town centre, Kirkwall, Orkney

Founded in 1137, the cathedral is one of the finest in Scotland and was completed about 1500. It is dedicated to St Magnus the Martyr, whose bones are buried within the church, and was founded by Earl Rognvald Kolson. It survived the Reformation intact.

Open all year except public holidays except Christmas festive season

P Nearby S

98 St Magnus Church, Egilsay

HY 467303 6 HS

West side of island of Egilsay, Orkney

The ruined church, dating from the 12th century, consists of a nave, square-ended chancel and round tower. Some have suggested that this was the church where Earl Magnus prayed before his murder by beheading around 1117. He was slain on the order of Earl Haakon, so that Haakon might rule in Orkney. Magnus was made a saint, and his bones were taken to St Magnus Cathedral in Kirkwall.

Open all year

99 St Margaret's Chapel, Edinburgh Castle
NT 252735   66   HS

Edinburgh Castle, Edinburgh

The oldest building in the castle, the small chapel was built by David I in the first half of the 12th century, and is dedicated to his mother, Saint Margaret. A fine Norman arch survives within the chapel. A copy of St Margaret's gospel book can be seen here.

☎ 0131 225 9846—Open all year

P Nearby (except during Edinburgh Festival)   ☕ S WC &
& Access

100 St Mary's Chapel, Crosskirk
ND 024700   12   HS

Off A836, 6 miles W of Thurso, Crosskirk, Caithness

The simple dry-stone chapel, probably built in the 12th century, is roofless but the walls are complete. The chapel probably had a thatched roof.

P Nearby

101 St Mary's Chapel, Rothesay
NS 086637   63   HS

On A845, 0.5 miles S of Rothesay Castle, Bute

The chapel, dedicated to St Mary and standing next to the parish church, may date from as early as the 13th century, and is all that remains of a larger building. The chapel was roofless, but is being restored. It houses two well-preserved tombs: one with the effigy of a warrior from the 14th century.

Open all year
P Nearby

102 St Mary's Church, Monymusk
NJ 684152   38

Off B993, Monymusk village

Standing on the site of an early Christian community, the nave, chancel arch and parts of the west tower date from 1170 when a priory of Augustinian canons was founded here. The priory was burnt in 1554, and much of the church dates from the 17th century and later. Housed in the church is the Monymusk Stone, a Pictish symbol stone; and the Monymusk Reliquary, which once held the bones of St Columba, was also kept here when it was a priory. The Reliquary was carried before Bruce's army at Bannockburn, and is now in the Royal Museum of Scotland.

 Nearby

103 St Mary's Church, Grandtully

NN 886505 52 HS

Off A827, 3 miles NE of Aberfeldy, Grandtully, Perthshire

Dating from the 16th century, St Mary's Church was re-modelled in 1633 when a finely painted ceiling illustrating heraldic and symbolic subjects was added.

104 St Mary's Collegiate Church, Haddington

NT 518736 66

Off A6093, Sidegate, Haddington, East Lothian

In a pleasant situation beside the River Tyne, St Mary's is a substantial 14th-century cruciform church with an aisled nave and choir, known as the Lamp of Lothian. It is the largest parish church in Scotland, and the roof is vaulted, apart from the restored nave. Marble monument to John

Maitland, Lord Thirlestane and Chancellor of Scotland, his wife and son, is now known as The Chapel of the Three Kings. Beneath lies the Lauderdale family vault. There are interesting medieval carvings around the church, including Green Men and scallop shells: a sign of pilgrimage.

Open daily April to September 11am-4.30pm; Sun 2-4pm

P Nearby 🍴 S wc 🦽 Access

105 St Mary's Parish Church, Whitekirk

NT 596815   67

On A198, Whitekirk, 3.5 miles SE of North Berwick, East Lothian

Dating from the 12th century with a 16th-century tower, the church was restored after being burnt in 1914 by suffragettes. Whitekirk was a place of pilgrimage in medieval times. It was visited by Aeneas Sylvius Piccolomini, later Pope Pious II, who after being saved from a storm walked barefoot to Whitekirk – and suffered rheumatism for the rest of his life. A fresco in the chapter house of Sienna Cathedral records his visit to Scotland. Tithe barn and historic graveyard.

Open all year

P Nearby S wc

106 St Michael's Church, Linlithgow

NT 003773   65

Off A803, near the Palace, Linlithgow, West Lothian

Founded in 1242 on the site of an earlier church, St Michael's dates

Cross-shaft, Pennygown (page 58)

mostly from the 15th century, although it now has an unfortunate steeple, added in 1964, to replace a stone crown such as at St Giles. Because of its proximity to the Palace, it has associations with the Stewart monarchs, in particular James IV and James V. There are interesting 15th-century relief slabs in the vestry.

Open all year Mon-Fri

P Nearby S

107 St Moluag's Church, Eorrapaidh

NB 519652 8

Off B8014 or B8013, Eorrapaidh, Ness, Isle of Lewis

Although there was probably a Christian site here from the 6th century, the present church dates from the 12th century. The existing church has round arched windows and door. An adjoining chapel, possibly used by

lepers, only has a squint – or viewing hole – into the main church. The building was restored in 1912, although it has no electricity or gas, and is lit by candles and lamps. Short walk to church.

Open Easter to 1st Sunday in September during daylight hours

P Nearby

108 St Monans Parish Church

NO 523014 59

Off A917, St Monans, Fife

Located in a impressive cliff-top location. Dating from 1370, the church was rib-vaulted in a cruciform plan with a central tower. In 1647 the choir was walled off and became ruinous, only to be restored in 1828 and again in 1961. The church houses a 14th-century sedilia, piscina, and aumbry, as well as medieval consecration crosses.

Open April-October during daylight hours

 S

109 St Ninian's Cave, Physgill

NX 421359 83 HS

Off A747, 4 miles SW of Whithorn, at Physgill, on coast

This cave is traditionally believed to be the retreat of St Ninian, whose *Candida Casa* was nearby at Whithorn, although the cave has partially collapsed. Crosses are carved on the walls, probably by pilgrims, and carved stones have also been found during excavations. Eleven stones, the carving dating from the 11th century or earlier, found here are now in the Whithorn museum.

Open all year – involves walk

110 St Ninian's Chapel, Isle of Whithorn

NX 479362 83 HS

Off A750, S end of village of Isle of Whithorn, Galloway

Occupying a site associated with St Ninian, the present ruined and roofless chapel dates from the 13th century, and occupies the site of an earlier building. It may have been used by pilgrims from Ireland and the Isle of Man on route to St Ninian's shrine at Whithorn.

Open all year – involves walk

111 St Nicholas Buccleuch Parish Church, Dalkeith
NT 330670   66

Off A68/A6094 junction, High Street, Dalkeith

Dedicated to St Nicholas, this medieval church became a collegiate
establishment in 1406, founded by Sir James Douglas. The nave and
transepts date from 1854, when the inside of the church was greatly
altered. The chancel was abandoned in 1590, walled off from the rest of
the church, and is now ruinous. Sir James Douglas, 1st Earl of Morton,
and his wife Joanna, daughter of James I, are buried in the choir and have
stone effigies.

Open Easter Sunday to 30 September weekdays 10-12pm and 2-
4pm, Sun 10-11am

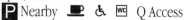 P Nearby ☕ ♿ WC Q Access

112 St Peter's Church, Duffus
NJ 175688   28   HS

Off B9102, Duffus, Moray

The roofless ruin consists of the base of a 14th-century tower – now the
Sutherland burial vault – and a fine 16th-century porch with a groined
vault, while the body of the church is 18th century. St Peter's Cross, a
typical medieval market cross – markets were held regularly in kirkyards
– and some good table-tombs survive in the churchyard.

Open all year

P Nearby

113 St Ternan's Church, Arbuthnott

NO 801746   45

Off B967, Arbuthnott, Aberdeenshire

The chancel of the present church dates from 1242, although an earlier church probably existed on the site, while the bell tower and west end were built about 1500. The church was gutted by fire in 1889, but was soon restored. In the Arbuthnott Aisle – formerly the Lady Chapel – is a 13th-century monument to Hugh Arbuthnott. Above the Arbuthnott Aisle is the Priest's Room, with stone window seats and a squint to the chapel.

Open all year

 Nearby   S   ♿ Limited Access

114 St Vigeans Church, Arbroath

NO 639429   54

Off A933, St Vigeans, 0.5 miles N of Arbroath, Angus

The church dates from the 12th century, and is dedicated to St Vigean, an Irish saint, who died in 664. A museum of early Christian and Pictish sculpture is housed in cottages nearby.

Open Sun in June – other times key available from house opposite church main gate

 Nearby   ☕

115 St Vigeans Sculptured Stones

NO 637430   54   HS

Off A933, St Vigeans village, 0.5 miles N of Arbroath

Fine collection of early Christian and Pictish stones housed in cottages.

Exhibition.

Open April to September – interesting church of St Vigeans nearby

 Nearby

116 Seton Collegiate Church

NT 418751 66 HS

On A198, 1.5 miles N of Tranent, East Lothian

Fine collegiate church, founded in 1492 by the 4th Lord Seton. The roof is vaulted, and transepts were added in the 16th century, as was a square rib-vaulted tower. Monuments survive within the church. Exhibition.

Open all year

P Nearby S £

117 Shandwick Cross-Slab

NH 855747 21

Off A9, about 6 miles S of Tain, Shandwick, Ross and Cromarty

Dating from the 8th or 9th century, the large cross-slab, known as Clach a'Charridh, stands about 9-feet high and stands in its original position. On one side is a prominent cross, below the arms are winged angels and other animal decoration. The other side has five panels, carved with figures, horsemen and animals.

Open all year

P Nearby

118 Stobo Kirk

NT 182376 72

Off B712, 4.5 miles SW of Peebles, Stobo, Borders

Dating from the 12th century, the nave and chancel of the Kirk are Norman, and a fine doorway survives within a 16th-century porch. The church was dedicated to St Mungo. The tower was altered in the 16th century, although the base is probably Norman. The church houses fine recumbent tombstones, and there are interesting 17th- and 18th-century gravestones in the churchyard.

Open all year

P Nearby & Limited Access

119 Sueno's Stone
NJ 046595   27   HS
Off A96, E side of Forres, Moray
Standing over 22-feet tall, this is the most
remarkable sculptured stone in Scotland,
dating from the 9th century. One main face is
carved with a large ring-headed cross, the
shaft of which is filled with interlaced
knotwork. The other is divided into four
panels which relate the events of a battle.
Open all year – protected (and obscured)
by glass enclosure

120 Sweetheart Abbey
NX 964663   84   HS
*On A710, in New Abbey, 6 miles S of
Dumfries, Dumfries and Galloway*
The fine and picturesque ruins of a 13th-
century Cistercian abbey, the church of which
is particularly well preserved while the cloister
and domestic buildings have mostly gone.
Much of the massive precinct wall survives.

Sueno's Stone

   The abbey was founded in 1273 by
Devorgilla of Galloway in memory of her
husband, John Balliol – they are both buried
here. Devorgilla kept the embalmed heart of
Balliol in a casket after his death in 1268 until her own in 1290. She was
the mother of John Balliol – *Toom Tabard* – John I, King of Scots. Her
headless effigy survives within the abbey.

   The abbey suffered at the hands of the English in the 13th and 14th
centuries, but it was dissolved at the Reformation, although Roman rites
were practised here until the 17th century.

☎ 01387 850397—Open April to September; joint entry ticket with
New Abbey Corn mill

 S £ ♿ Access

Teampull na Trionaid

121 Teampull na Trionaid

NF 816602   22

On A865, Carinish, North Uist

Teampull na Trionaid, dedicated to the Trinity, dating from the 13th or
14th century, was one of the largest pre-Reformation churches in the
Western Isles. It is said to have been built by Amie MacRurie, first wife of
John, Lord of the Isles. The church is now very ruined, although the
adjoining chapel is in a better condition, and the buildings are to be
consolidated. Teampull na Trionaid was probably an important centre of
learning and teaching in medieval times.

Open all year—beware of a possible slaister of mud

P Nearby

122 Torphichen Preceptory

NS 968725   65   HS

Off B792, in Torphichen, West Lothian

The Preceptory was the Scottish seat of the Knights Hospitallers or
Knights of St John of Jerusalem. The surviving nave, transepts and choir
were built by the 13th century, although little of the domestic buildings
or cloister survive. Within the churchyard, stands a cross-inscribed stone,

believed to mark the centre of the sanctuary ground – there were four other stones. The Preceptory was dissolved during the Reformation, and part of the building is now used as the parish church.

View from exterior

 Nearby

123 Trumpan Church

NG 225613   23

Off B886, Trumpan, Skye

The ruined shell of a medieval church, which had a thatched roof. A raiding party of MacDonalds slaughtered the MacLeod congregation while at worship one Sunday in 1578 by setting fire to the thatch. One woman escaped and raised the alarm, and in retaliation the raiding party was exterminated to a man by the MacLeods from Dunvegan Castle.

  Near the church is the Trial Stone, which has a small hole in it near the top. The trial was carried out by blindfolding the accused, who would be proved to be telling the truth if they succeeded in putting their finger in the hole at the first time of trying.

Open all year

124 Tullibardine Chapel

NN 909134   58   HS

Off A823, 6 miles SE of Crieff, Perthshire

Unaltered small medieval church, founded in 1446, although rebuilt about 1500. One of the most complete examples of a small collegiate church in Scotland. Exhibition.

Open April to September

125 Whithorn Priory

NX 444403   83   HS

On A746 in Whithorn, Dumfries & Galloway

The site of a 5th-century Christian community of St Ninian, who built a stone church here, dedicated to St Martin of Tours. The church was white-washed and was known as *Candida Casa* – 'White House', and its location was probably within the present ruined church. Nothing definite

remains from this period except carved stones

Whithorn was a popular place of pilgrimage in medieval times. The existing ruins are of a 12th-century Premonstratensian priory and cathedral: the nave of the Romanesque church survives although it is unroofed. The vaulted chambers under the nave also remain, and probably housed the shrine of St Ninian.

The church continued to be used both as a cathedral and a parish church after the Reformation, and was not abandoned until 1822 when the nearby modern church was built on the east side of the cloister.

A fine collection of early Christian sculpture is housed in the nearby museum, including the *Latinus Stone*, the earliest Christian memorial in Scotland; the *St Peter's Stone*; and the 10th-century Monreith Cross, which is carved with interlaced patterns and has a round head. Visitor centre. Exhibition.

☎ 01988 500508—Open March to October; ruins of Priory open all year

P Nearby ⌖ ♿ Limited access

Glossary

Abbey	Monastery headed by an abbot
Abbot	Head of abbey of monks or canons
Aisle	Outer part of body of church, separated by an arcade of pillars
Apse	Semi circular or polygonal east end of church, contained altar
Arcade	Row of arches
Aumbry	Recess for storing books, vessels
Bishop	Head of church diocese
Calefactory	The warming house, only room in monasteries which was heated
Campanile	Bell-tower
Canon	Member of order of priests serving cathedral or abbey
Chancel	Eastern end of church used by clergy and choir
Chantry	Small endowed chapel, used to say masses for the dead
Chapter-house	Meeting room used to discuss business of monastic chapter; burial place of abbots
Chevrons	Zig-zag carving, ornamental feature of Norman (Romanesque) architecture

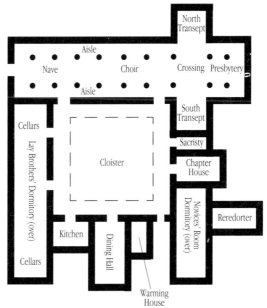

Medieval monastery – showing common elements

Choir   Part of chancel used by priests and singers
Cinquefoil   Cusped decoration, divides arch or circle into five parts
Clerestory   Upper windows over aisles
Cloister   Rectangular area around which monastic buildings were located
Collegiate church   Church which had college of priests but no bishop
Commendator   Person holding revenues of abbey, was not always a
                 churchman
Crossing   Part of church where nave, chancel and transepts intersect
Cruciform church   Cross-shaped church, transepts form shape of cross
Crypt   Basement area, often vaulted, sometimes used for burials

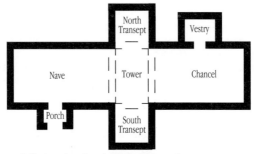

Collegiate church – showing common elements

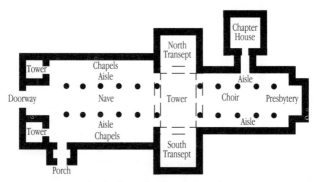

Medieval cathedral – showing common elements

Medieval parish church – showing common elements

Day stair	To the dormitory from the cloister, used during the day
Diocese	Territory served by cathedral and bishop
Dormitory or dorter	Sleeping accomodation
Effigy	Bronze or stone figure on tomb, usually horizontal
Font	Ceremonial baptism basin
Frater	Monastic dining area or refectory
Friars	Religious brothers, bound by vows, but not confined to monasteries
Gargoyle	Ornate water spout
Gothic	Pointed-arch style of architecture, introduced mid 12th century
Grange	Monastic farm lands
Infirmary	Building where the sick were cared for
Kirk	Church (Scotland)
Lavatorium	Washing area
Lectern	Reading desk
Manse	Minister's house
Misericord	Ledge found in stalls, which was used to provide some rest for older or infirm clergy, during long periods of standing during services. Often highly decorated
Monastery	Group of buildings which housed a community of monks, canons or nuns
Nave	Area of church where congregation stood
Night stair	From the dormitory to church, used for night services
Norman	Round-arched style of architecture c11th and 12th centuries, (Romanesque)
Parlour	Room where monks were permitted to talk
Piscina	Basin in wall, used to wash communion vessels
Precinct	The grounds around monastery, enclosed by boundary wall
Presbytery	East part of church; the priest's quarters; or post-Reformation level of church administration between kirk and synod
Priory	Monastery headed by a prior, less important that an abbey
Quire	Alternative spelling for choir
Reformation	Change in church organisation and doctrine, essentially rejection of the authority of Rome by Protestants
Reredorter	Latrine block connected to dormitory
Romanesque	Round-arched style of architecture c11th and 12th centuries, (Norman)
Rood	Crucifix, cross
Rood screen	Screen between chancel and nave, often carved, separating clergy from congregation
Sacrament house	Ornate cupboard for storing sacrament
Sacristy	Room where sacred vessels and vestments stored (vestry)
Sedilia	Seats in the chancel, usually in threes, for priests
Shrine	Contained saint's body or relics

A Wee Guide to Old Churches and Abbeys of Scotland

Slype   Passage out of cloister
Stalls   Seats for singers or dignitaries
Stoup   Basin for holy water, found at entrance to church
Teinds   Tenth part of household goods, paid to the church in kind
Tracery   Intersected ribwork found in later Gothic windows
Trefoil   Three-lobed decoration
Undercroft Basement or crypt
Yett   Gate

Christian Communities

MONASTIC ORDERS

Celtic monasticism – introduced at Iona by Irish monks under Columba about 563. Essentially hermits who lived isolated, ascetic lives in individual cells located around communal oratory.

Benedictine Order – founded about 530 at Monte Cassino, by St Benedictine of Nursia. Much later a united network of abbeys was created. Seven Benedictine abbeys found in Scotland. Dunfermline was the most important Benedictine abbey in Scotland.

Cluniac Order – reformed order of Benedictines. Attempted to re-establish a stricter form of monasticism. Abbey founded at Cluny, France in 909 and later formed a separate order of monasteries. Three Cluniac houses founded in Scotland. Both the worship and the buildings of this order would eventually become extremely elaborate, despite their initial attempts at simplicity. Crossraguel abbey, a Cluniac abbey, was founded in 1214 by Duncan, 1st Earl of Carrick.

Tironensian Order – founded in France by St Bernard of Tiron in 1109 as a reformed Benedictine order. First foundation in Scotland, and Britain, was at Selkirk, 1113, by David I. Later order moved to Kelso, and a further seven houses were established throughout Scotland. Arbroath abbey is the best surviving example of a Tironensian abbey.

Cistercian Order – another reformed Benedictine order. Founded by St Robert of Molesme at Cîteaux in France, in 1098. St Bernard insisted that the monastic buildings should be plain and built away from towns and population settlements. Introduced, also by David I, at Melrose in 1136. Later 12 abbeys established in Scotland. Melrose and Sweetheart are the two best surviving examples.

Valliscaulian Order – reformed order, although formed much later. Mother house was at Val de Choux, in France, and first reached Scotland in 1230. Three Scottish priories founded. The remains of Ardchattan and Beauly can be visited, the priory at Beauly is now a Benedictine abbey and is open to the public.

ORDERS OF CANONS

Augustinian Canons – earliest house founded at Scone in 1120 by Alexander I. Later about 18 houses established. The abbeys of Inchcolm and Jedburgh, and the priory at Inchmahome, are all interesting examples of Augustinian houses.

Premonstratensian Canons – founded in France by St Norbert of Xanten, at Prémontré, in 1120. Ascetic order of canons, similar to Cistercian order of monks. Likely to have been introduced at Dryburgh, and a further five houses were founded in Scotland. Both Dryburgh abbey and the priory at Whithorn have substantial remains.

Trinitarian Canons – had eight houses in Scotland. At the Cross Kirk in Peebles are the ruins and foundations of the Trinitarian priory founded in 1474, the only surviving house of this order.

ORDERS OF FRIARS

Dominican Friars – known as Blackfriars, established by St Dominic at Toulouse, France, in 1215. First reached Scotland in 1230.

Franciscan Friars – known as Greyfriars, were established by St Francis in 1215. Reached Scotland about 1231. Both orders became linked with the newly-formed universities which appeared in the 13th century.

ORDERS OF KNIGHTS

Knights Hospitallers – or Knights of the Hospital of St John, founded in the 12th century to provide care for sick and poor, and to provide safe escort to the Holy Land. They followed the Augustinian order and were introduced to Scotland by David I about 1144. The preceptory at Torphichen was the Scottish headquarters of the order.

Knights Templars – another military order also introduced by David I. In 1312 the order was suppressed by the Pope and their property passed to the Knights Hospitallers. Although there was a preceptory at Temple, little remains of the original buildings.

Index